River Diary

RIVER DIARY

RONALD BLYTHE

CANTERBURY
PRESS
Norwich

© Ronald Blythe 2008

First published in 2008 by the
Canterbury Press Norwich
(a publishing imprint of Hymns Ancient & Modern
Limited, a registered charity)
13–17 Long Lane, London EC1A 9PN

www.scm-canterburypress.co.uk

Second impression

British Library Cataloguing in Publication data

A catalogue record for this book is available
from the British Library

ISBN 978-1-85311-862-3

Typeset by Rowland Phototypesetting Ltd,
Bury St Edmunds, Suffolk
Printed and bound in Great Britain by
MPG Books Ltd, Bodmin, Cornwall

Contents

In Memoriam
PAUL TAYLOR
Wissington – the Western Desert

Acknowledgement

These entries are from the *Word from Wormingford* column in *Church Times*.

Foreword

These pages first saw light in the *Church Times*, 2005–7. They are more a soliloquy on than a history of those recent years, made so by the passing of old friends. To give the Vicar and our hard-working rulers their due, not everyone is as tentatively engaged in life as myself. You have only to read our magazine *The Worm*. And there were dramas which must await the short story or even the novel. It was famously wet, though nothing in the way of floods. And I finished a book called *Field Work*, never went anywhere particularly, and mourned Jane Garrett and Roger Deakin. As for the River Stour, it took not the least bit of notice.

Ronald Blythe
August 2007

Going to Meet Captain Jones

New Year's Day

The Epiphany. Isaiah's 'multitude of camels and dromedaries of Midian' join Reginald Heber's 'beasts of the stall'. We say together, 'Arise, shine, for thy light is come . . . and the Gentiles shall come to that light, and the kings to the brightness of thy rising. Lift up thy eyes round about, and see!' Stephen and I are lifting our eyes up round Harwich where oyster-catchers feed on the seaweed. Across an all but washed-away breakwater I catch a glimpse of Dr Johnson stomping to and fro as the ship carrying his new young friend James Boswell makes for Holland. We turn the corner and there before us is Captain Christopher Jones's house, a trim building with over-sailing and four handsome sash windows, and quite decent a home to be the birthplace of the sailor who had the nerve (and the payment) to take a somewhat decrepit vessel named *Mayflower* into world history. His wife Josian had a quarter share in it. No doubt the hundred exactly passengers, plus their beasts of the stall and their seedcorn, had given over a tidy sum for the two-month voyage. Less than four years later this same ship would lie in ruins at Rotherhithe, its planks running with mud and gulls.

Harwich is still heavy with Christmas. Faces peer out at us from poky pubs. Like the *Mayflower*, the little port itself had fallen apart right up until the 1960s. As a boy I found it quite sensationally tumbledown, like one of those W. W. Jacobs places in which seamen and their friends were huggermugger, beckoning, and out of my own world. But then arrived the container-ships, the EU, the spruced-up Trinity House, the luxurious ferry, and the rescue of the ancient streets. This last included the just-in-time salvation of the 1911 Electric Palace cinema outside of which Stephen and I lurked for a moment as we imagined Buster Keaton unsmiling through the cigarette-fog, and the lady crashing away at the piano.

The harbour light on this Epiphany is like that of Delft, milkily blue but touched with a rich dull gold. A listless tide slops against the moorings. The red brick lighthouse, stolen from a Vermeer, rears above us, as do the fine section houses which the Norwegians gave to Harwich after the devastating 1953 flood. We might be where the Stour pours into the North Sea, yet we feel that we are not quite in England. Yet Samuel Pepys was its MP. And everyone who was anyone stepped ashore here or sailed away here. Driving home, we say thank you to Harwich for blowing the Christmas cobwebs away. The Essex interior is flat and sullen as the day fades. The 1930s ribbon development peters out and leaves behind that special kind of emptiness which trails behind the coast. Here and there in a garish window Santa Claus continues to be merry. Back home the cards will be toppling about on the bookcase and dead holly will be crinkling on the beams. And Isaiah is saying, 'Surely the isles shall wait for me, and the ships of Tarshish first, to bring thy sons from afar, their silver and their gold with them . . . and a little one shall become a thousand.'

Stephen gone, I read my presents by the light of the new desk-lamp which unfortunately appeals to the vanity of the white cat, who knows how lovely she looks when sprawled under it. Thus about two feet of purring fur intrudes on to the page. The book is Graham Parry's *The Arts of the Anglican Counter-Reformation*. Never before could they have been so intelligently described, all that then contentious furniture which we now polish, the fittings of George Herbert's *Temple*.

Look Away Now

7th January

One of World War Two's finest poems is Henry Reed's 'Naming of Parts'. Is it a masterpiece of inattention or a lesson on true values? The soldier poet attends the rifle class but is diverted by what is happening in the garden outside. The instructor says, as he slides the bolt backwards and forwards, 'We call this easing the spring', whilst beyond the window, beyond the war itself, 'The early bees are assaulting and fumbling the flowers: / They call it easing the Spring'. The inattentive poet is young but with old age there comes a similarly powerful distraction known as contemplation. The parishes are in one of their perennial uproars over theme parks, rubbish dumps, church lavatories; and dramatic though these things are, try as one would, it is impossible to keep them at the front of one's mind. A friend in her nineties declines to come to church after eighty years' attendance. She doesn't even feel any further need of the Sacraments. What her heart tells her is, 'Be still'. How valuable it is during the last years to alter one's attention – not that one has much choice in the matter. Before today's retirement requirements, it was normal for a parish to have an old priest who was helplesly distracted by contemplation, and here I am not giving some kind of mental decline a kindly label. Little was done and because of this much was done.

Well, I haven't quite reached this stage, and the 'dream-boat' part of me with which I have been tagged since boyhood hasn't quite sailed out of sight, but religiously I do increasingly drift, shall we say. When W. H. Auden was old he found himself 'caring less and less for more and more'. The huge caring for a world hit by fascism had in fact, and due to his brave poetry, done wonders, and now he rightly believed that he should retreat (go forward) into the Anglican quiet of his family. So doing, he became the very epitome of sloth. But how he delighted in this late vision of his. Not many of his friends understood that he was not a free agent – that God was taking up his time to a large extent.

Acts of contemplation are more regularly witnessed in city churches than country churches. Sometimes in London I find myself contemplating the contemplators, discreetly, lovingly. The large black woman, the smart office worker, the beautiful girl with her closed laptop, the youth who may be sheltering from the streets. There they sit in the lunch-hour, good as gold, and so evidently precious in God's sight. You rarely see such worship in our village churches where out-of-service attenders have either a Pevsner or a watering-can in their hands. The time will come – it is irresistible in the long run – when all that matters is the uncluttered business known as being still in the ultimate Presence, a perfectly-at-ease state where language need not intrude although it is a help to have the trees muttering in the churchyard.

However, I stray from the point. These city contemplatives of mine, the watchers out for God being watched, are at that stage of life when one chooses to allow its noisy demands to slip, for the lunch-hour at least. Whereas the contemplative of the last years has no option but to look out of the window when people rush at him with petitions against, or for, this and that to demonstrate the practical workings of existence. How cross the young neighbours of the ancient Apostle John were when all he could tell them was, 'Little children, love one another.'

Warm Winters

14th January

'What we need is a good hard frost', says the unknown rider as she squelches up the track, her horse's hooves imprinting watery cicatrices in the mud. 'Yes,' I say supinely, for to be honest I find the warm January days blissful. I too squelch from bed to bed, from bush to tree whilst a blackbird sings aloft and unseasonal zephyrs mark my way as in a Handel opera. Snowdrops prick the earth and a couple of primroses are actually out. The air is brand-new from whichever quarter it mildly blows. I thought I might walk to the church and ask the young pointer of pinnacles if he knew that mortar was once strengthened with 'malt liquor'. I must also enquire of the poet James Knox Whittet, late of Islay, and a welcome visitor to Bottengoms, whether he had heard of this use of his island's main export. He may well blanch at the thought of a single malt holding a church tower together.

But 'good hard frosts', snowfalls and bitter north winds, and Robin trying to keep himself warm, poor thing, will they be no more? Don't count on it. Little Ice Age or global warming, winter wild will come again. So make the most of a tropical January. The happiness of a bedroom window gaping across the fields all night and a cat asleep in the in-tray all day. The pleasure of the ditches rippling away, not with frigid gushes from the field-drains but with a sparkle. Sorting the Christmas cards into piles of needing a reply and not needing a reply. I spend some time admiring the pictures. Hardly any Pickwickian coaches, but quite a few Dutch villagers dancing about on the snow. And who would want to stay inside during the little Ice Age without window-panes? Just shutters, and these blowing open. So put on every garment you possess and frolic by the river, play football – a favourite pitch was the frozen river – and drink a malt or two and by no means let the builder have it for bodging the cracks in the church.

Just twice have I been snowed-up down at the farmhouse. The first time I opened the front door on to a snow buttress and couldn't get out. And both times it was impossible to get up the track to the lane, a distance of about a mile, due to a filling-in with snowdrifts. The neighbours – people in this country always become frenzied during a big snowfall – were amazed that my telephone still worked and said that they placed food at the top 'if you can get to it'. In vain did I describe my deep freeze with its many packages bossily lettered, some of them, 'expiry date 1997' etc., and my laid-out apples, and my shelf-ful of jams and pickles, although I do not tell them about the wine as I have to preserve some kind of sobriety in my position. These epic snowfalls knew that an ancient house had to have some kind of drama in its long life. Had it not endured several centuries of the little Ice Age? One of them sans glass windows? Had not its thatch kept snug under a ton of snow and its eaves hung with icicles, and its inhabitants in January rushed from it into the cosy garden? Dark, dark it would have been, those Ice Age Epiphnies. And yet light. Not much light where that religious mob outside Parliament was concerned. And how British that their sacred fury should turn on the moral argument of a B and B. Such a nation has nothing to fear.

To Mount Bures for Epiphany Matins and to daydream in that spiry little place and listen to the softly battering wind during the Lessons. We sing *Cantate Domino* – 'then shall all the trees of the wood rejoice before the Lord'. And it is so.

Michael Mayne

1st February

I suppose that the memorial service is not always necessary nor desirable, that formal *L'envoi* after the huge poem of the funeral. And where it is essential the dead themselves should make it in order to avoid the polite praise of the living. So what to expect in Westminster Abbey as we wait for the service to begin? It is the first of February, a spring in winter noon with the sunshine whirling through the Rose window and making the Apostles giddy. Purbeck columns, usually a moody blue, flare into space. Just behind me, glimpsed over my shoulder, all the poets look warm to the touch. Introit after introit fills the building like an unavoidable grace, and our whispers, like wind in poplars, rustle through them as we settle to hear what Michael has to say for himself. One of his difficulties will be that, having had such a passion for this life, will he be able to reveal an equivalent comprehension of what has to succeed it? Well, we will see, or rather hear. Meanwhile, the delectable moment before the procession appears.

Of course the memorial service will be one of Michael's knowledgeable anthologies – how could it be otherwise? It will be about death and leaving and arriving, about his passing and our passing, and about his loving everything en route and about our need to love everything on the way. When I stayed with him at Westminster Deanery it was like being with a heavenly geographer. He was so appreciative! One of the things which God is bound to ask us, after the funeral, and maybe the memorial service, is, 'Why didn't you simply *enjoy* my beautiful creation?' Michael and I would talk of Traherne, that Christian earth-enjoyer without peer. And now we are singing Timothy Dudley-Smith's *Magnificat*, unnumbered blessings giving our spirits voice, and now we are hearing one of the finest descriptions of death in literature as Bunyan's pilgrim hears what we hear when the doctor announces our mortality. What Michael heard, and with what interest! Bunyan's pilgrim is Mr Valiant-for-Truth for whom the trumpets sounded on the other side. Bunyan used whatever came to hand for death and life. The Great Ouse flowed below his prison cell. A Bedford trumpeter blew curfew each night on its bridge. Michael Mayne was a great man for making connections and drawing conclusions. At his self-devised memorial service he connects where the connection has been broken or long ignored. It is what he did in life. He was a great Christian anthologist who drew us towards poets who were articulate on all things and once shown to us by him, proved to be memorably so. He was good on fear.

'I have formerly lived by hear-say and faith, but now I go where I shall live by sight, and shall be with him, in whose company I delight myself . . . wherever I have seen the print of his shoe in the earth, there I have coveted to set my foot too.'

The Church is always talking about its 'resources' whilst undervaluing its true resources, and undervaluing its inherited language, especially the prose and poetry of death. We say the General Confession, we sing hymns as they should be sung, moved to unfamiliar tears at times. Poets' Corner listens, or maybe joins in. Afterwards Michael's family stands on one side of the Unknown Warrior and the clergy on the other, and we queue to embrace. Beyond the west door London is white and gold, pre-tourist and rather un-busy.

How to Paint Towers

4th February

Cathedrals disturb our journeys. Who has not glanced up from a book on the train as it rushes past Durham or creeps into Ely and not only lost his place but his way? Throughout his life Claude Monet would leave Paris or his beloved Giverny to visit his father at Le Havre or his brother at Rouen, following the Seine all the route. In February 1892 he put up at an hotel whose windows faced the south-west front of Rouen Cathedral. Its immense tower with its needle-like spire, a fairly recent addition, could not be seen, cut off as it were by glazing-bars. Watching the daylight falling in continually altering hues on the grand entrance, shifting from viewpoint to viewpoint, he conceived an extraordinary set of pictures, thirty in all, which would record what happened to a building every hour. Thus one of the mightiest painterly concepts was achieved. It was the Irish writer George Moore who described Impressionism as 'the rapid noting of elusive appearance'. Thus Monet's *Cathedrals*, as these studies came to be called, which took him ten hours a day over nearly two years to complete, are something other than Impressionistic. Suffice to see them as perfect statements on what atmosphere hourly does to stone.

This climatic vision of both architecture and its local land-scape wasn't new. John Constable understood it all his life and called it 'a science'. But it was left to Monet at the close of the nineteenth century to make this astonishing statement on it by showing Rouen Cathedral round the clock. He caused paint to give the time of day to a building, one which the viewer could almost set his watch by. He entitled his studies *Early afternoon; 2–3 pm*, etc. And it was exactly that. Constable called his painting of a cart and horse standing quiet and still in the millpond *Noon* but a friend dubbed it *The Haywain*. Artists like to give their world the time of day.

A monolithic church tower catches every light there is as I walk down my farm track. It is that of Stoke-by-Nayland church. It rises from a hill five miles off and for a minute or two it is framed by an oak and an ash before it vanishes altogether. I know exactly where to catch it as I bring down the paper and the milk, but I cannot 'know' its infinite variety, only marvel at its pinks and bloody reds, its translucent solidarity, its ability sometimes to be as golden as St Bernard's Jerusalem, or as gossamer as dragonflies' wings. Like Monet at Rouen, Constable painted it over and over again, once when the labourers were rioting, chalking-in a rainbow over its pinnacles, a symbol of the divine providence. This tower is 120 feet high. We climbed it as boys, praying that Canon Clibbon wouldn't catch us, or worse his verger. 'Come you down you little B's!' We wanted to see Harwich Water from the top. It was up and up and round and round, the tower's dusty entrails clunking and groaning, and a strange interior wind hooting at us and, worst of all, the bellringers starting up to deafen us like poor Quasimodo, the hunchback of Notre Dame.

We were in Stoke again last week, to find them clearing trees and 'rubbish' (wild plants) in order to let us see the tower from where Constable saw it. We made a pilgrimage to the south doors, a pair of tall silvery-grey carvings of amazing beauty, weathered by Suffolk hands, weighing a ton yet light as air. Doors which Constable's painty fingers would have opened. He and Monet let us view architecture in all the dispensations of daylight.

Now the floodlight sponsors of Stoke-by-Nayland tower – £6 at the Post Office – allow us night vision of its magnificence. During the last week of the old year 'Philip, so loved', and 'Wendy, Nicolette and James, the best family anyone could wish for', are celebrated. Their names fill the niches left empty by topped saints and crowd the shields of forgotten lords. 'You have kept the church lit,' says the magazine. So have we, says the sun and rain, the mists and winds. Seeing Stoke touch the sky, Constable reminds it, 'I am the man of clouds'. Seeing Rouen that early afternoon, Monet told his wife, 'Every day it is whiter; more and more it is blazing straight down . . .'. Church towers, what are they really for if not to raise our sights?

Dressing Down

16th February

I am ironing my gardening clothes, having scrubbed them, and should guests be present, to their derision. Life is divided between ironers and non-ironers. I am also attending Melvyn's morning class. This week – Archimedes. Where else in all the wide broadcasting universe could one listen to such a programme? Outside, a faint fall of snow is evaporating under the sun. The sun is throwing its golden weight about this winter. Birds sit in the snow in order to capture my concern. 'Look at us!' they squeak, 'in the deep mid-winter, snow on snow' – that kind of thing. But even as they speak their warm bodies melt the few flakes and they are bobbing about on spring grass. I scatter it with crumbled cream crackers. They tell God about my charity. I listen to a woodpecker on a nearby dead elm, a fine drummer. The elms have returned, but only for about twenty feet, when they perish and turn a grey-silver in the field hedges. Grubs then take them over and they become woodpeckers' breakfast bars.

No actual holes in the gardening jersey and jeans, the cosy jacket, but some thinning where my joints are, some transparency about the knees. Some presence of seeds in the pockets. Melvyn's brilliant guests have got to the part where Archimedes has to examine the king's golden crown for authenticity. He has ordered it from the best goldsmith but there is something fishy about it, or rather silvery. Has he passed it off as 22 carat when in fact it is partly silver? Ask Archimedes. Then we come to the best bit, but the experts are somewhat cool about Archimedes jumping out of his bath and shouting, 'Eureka!' Why, anyway, was he worrying his head over such things as his body being an irregular solid? And why the volume of an irregular solid could be calculated by measuring the water it displaced when it was immersed? I tell my friends to be careful not to run big baths at the farmhouse. They are not in London now. Too much water and the pump starts up. Though what if it does? Isn't this what a pump is for? But ancient pump facts have been bred in me and although they are now obsolete I continue to honour them. I possess a kind of congenital austerity which is shocked when people wash up a few cups under a running tap or fill the bath. Melvyn's guests are undermining this. One thing the Eureka story proves is that Archimedes had a private tub and did not have to join the rest of the community at the Syracuse public baths. Imagine having to get all those bodies out before being able to shout, 'Eureka!'

The newspaper arrives and here is a bad-tempered youth modelling my gardening clothes, the coat costing £10,000, the trousers only £850. He wears an unironed shirt which has been designed to go straight from its maker to Oxfam. And here is Finance and Business with rows of lords with old faces and dividential thinking written on them, and of course one cannot stop thinking about the poor young man who was advised to give all his money away. And I wonder which section Archimedes would have been in, the Fitted Bathrooms or the Crime, his running down the street naked and crying, 'Eureka!' Outside, the primroses are edged with snow, the hellebores, called thus because they are of uncertain origin, like most of us, are magnificent, and the hazel catkins are profuse. They said that Archimedes was so busy inventing things that he didn't know what was happening. And who does – exactly?

Cedd's Essex Adventure

24th February

Wild, wet, mild days, perfect weather for taking cuttings. The fields are lakes, the lanes stream. But the skies, such chasing glories, such empires of the clouds. Everything is watery or aerial movement. Birds sing loudly, willows green, cars are amphibious, shoes useless, gutters gurgle. Lent is a marsh, not a desert. The village churches are scrubbed and polished, and squelchy to approach. How the dead shine! The Ash Wednesday ashes run on my forehead. 'Blow the trumpet in Zion, sanctify a fast, call a solemn assembly . . . let the priests, the minister of the Lord, weep between the porch and the altar', I tell the damp congregation. Lying in bed in the ancient room I listen to the rain's silvery drip from tile to tile.

On Saturday to Chelmsford Cathedral, that warm-hearted place, to receive The Order of St Cedd and to sing Evensong to Dyson in D, and to install new canons. It is both grand and simple, as well as overwhelming when the choir arrives at Parry's 'I was glad when they said unto me'. It is one of those high formalities of Anglicanism which touch the heart. I think of Cedd standing under a dripping oak, his yellow Saxon hair, short in the front, long at the back, lank on his shoulders, careful not to get his Gospel soaked. They had sent him from Lindisfarne to convert his own people in their forest clearings and coastal saltings. The latter is where he found the Count of the Saxon Shore's abandoned fort and made it his base. It was from there he walked to spread a beautiful Celtic Christianity from tree to tree. The East Saxons were in the religious dumps due to 'wyrd' or fatalism. Then here comes this young man with a painted book and their king's blessing, and a tale of hope, to turn their lives upside down. Two of his preaching trees remain, one at Great Yeldham and one at Polstead. I have stood beneath both. The Yeldham tree is corseted by iron hands made by the blacksmith. Long dead, it cannot tumble down. The Polstead oak did fall, but a sapling has sprung from it. Cedd and the Celtic missionaries were not woodlanders, of course, but shore men. They liked the noise which the seashore perpetually makes. Sea-sounds were the concomitant of Celtic prayer. Without sea-cadence, prayer to them sounded thin. For St Cuthbert, the sea's call was as necessary as the office bell. Writing about Cuthbert, Bede said:

Down he went towards the beach . . . and out into the see until he was up to his arms and neck in deep water. The splash of the waves accompanied his vigil throughout the dark hours of the night. At daybreak he came out and knelt down on the sand, and prayed. Then two otters bounded out of the water, stretched themselves out before him, warmed his feet with their breath, and tried to dry him on their fur . . .

Giving a poetry reading in Cedd's gaunt church by the Bradwell sea I heard gulls scrambling and wailing in the roof. Naturally one would miss this kind of choir in a wood, these sacred screams, this restlessness of birds.

Tracking

26th February

P roust's novels *Swann's Way* and *The Guermantes Way* were no more than the brief country walks which people had to take in order to get out of their towns and villages. Trodden countless times in a lifetime, they would eventually provide a kind of dream route for the local person who had to travel them. Bunyan, recognising that the Puritan work ethic had taken over the old spring pilgrimages, suggested that the daily way to toil could be a form of meditation, and I have no doubt that it was. Passing and re-passing the same objects for years often sets the imagination free, particularly when a compulsory tramp is done in solitude. He wrote a little book called *The Heavenly Footman* which had nothing to do with servitude.

Lent is when I do more than walk my track. To the top and back again is a mile and a half of flinty travel accompanied by birdsong. Also, should I be in my historical mood, by ghosts. Saxon farmers, medieval children, Georgian parsons, poor Victorian labourers and the youthful versions of some of the old friends who sit before me in church. Who planted the twelve tall oaks just after Trafalgar? Who climbed the vast split oak just after Marston Moor? Who picked the bluebells which are now just showing? Who lay in the hollows with whom? That would be telling. Footpaths lead to private experience, main roads to public happenings. Which is why we are advised to stick to the narrow way. Let the high banks enfold you, let the rain hollows splash you. Let the occasional fellow traveller give you no more than a nod, the pair of you being at your devotions.

The rivulet side of Bottengoms track would have been animated by hedgers and ditchers in February, but that was long ago. Now the elder twists and tumbles, the hazels make forests and the brambles impenetrable cages for rabbits. Arching trees make a stately entrance, after which there comes an airy humdrum scene of open cornfield and horse paddocks. Then often neglected but beseeching signs of 'Cars turn here' and 'MUD'. For the slough of despond stretches between me and Garnon's Farm, the dull brasses of whose medieval owners hang under the belfry. Optimistic young men in vans believe that they can get through but soon they are knocking on the door, contrite and amazed, and there are directions to the RAC on how to find the track. I see wagons and carts and maybe a smart gig containing a lady, all getting through with a bit of a slide here and there, and squelching hooves and a 'gittup!', and an all is well. And the ditchers glancing up at slivers of sky, and the February day dragging on, and their legs in sodden sacking, and what would now be done in an hour with a dredger, taking weeks. What is this? we might enquire, staring at this winter world. The answer is, a handmade landscape for us to wander in and contemplate our lot.

At weekends the young commuter families and their dogs walk it. They pause at the floods of snowdrops in my wood and look glad to have made the move. The footpath, they slowly realise, belongs to them. Wherever we stroll, the way belongs to us. At this moment it is our way. It converses with us at every step. It makes us fanciful and serious all at once. And then there is botany, of course. Who can miss it on a track? And there is perpetual skylark music from on high, and the postman coming down at a fair lick, and the old struggle and the old distances.

Map-readings

1st March

A blissful spring in winter day. An hour of light snow and a morning of pale sunshine. Grey ice, thin as paper, on the puddles. Seedheads rattling against each other to keep themselves warm. Five pheasants in the dip. The church clock telling the hours piercingly. Wild daffodils, the ones which Dorothy Wordsworth noted for William, high up in the orchard mulch. The stream clear and hurrying. Gerald the shop dog bouncing through the goal-posts. The sky a pearly buff with sudden starlings darkening its edges. A walker's day, a wanderer's day. Thus bereft voices on the answer-phone. 'We tried to get you.'

One thing leading to another, such as spring-cleaning, the climate being contrary, I turn out the map drawer, having already turned out the sock drawer. The latter is a great mystery. Eight single socks. How can that be? And some vast knitted socks from the Ice Age. And some nice tennis socks, very fetching. And no darned socks, these now being in the museum. But maps. It was a casual studying of John Speed's *Atlas of Wales* which led me to the map drawer. John Speed was a Cheshire tailor who died in 1629 but he was mad on maps and mapping. While acknowledging the great map-makers Norden and Saxton – 'I have put my sickle into other mens corne' – his marvellous *Theatre of the Empire of Great Britaine*, which is what he called his maps, is very much his own. He was often not very well as he got about, which may be why his Wales shows his exasperation with its 'uneavenness'. The air on Anglesey is 'reasonably grateful' and that is about all. But oh the maps drawn by John Sudbury and George Humbell, one could look at them for ever, with their grand cartouches and endless humps – 'the tops whereof, in the Summer time, are the harvestmen's Almanacks'. I look up Discoed, where I go every September, pop. 60, or thereabouts, and there it is.

The map drawer doesn't stop here. Reading a map whilst in motion causes an acute anxiety. Reading one when one is still is sheer happiness. Some of my maps have been read to tatters. Some, being pre-motorway, would get you lost in no time. Each is a work of art, a dream, a reality, a will-o-the-wisp, an essential need and a distraction. They whiff of ancient car-pockets, grass and destinations. See how they bend. See how Norfolk has fallen in the sea. But see too how beautiful the new ones are, how they make you want to set off this very minute to that village where there wasn't time to stop or that street with the bookshop. I have come a roundabout journey to the map drawer, one directed by my Sunday sermon about Jack Kerouac and Jesus being 'on the road', the writer discovering a by-path, the Saviour being a 'way' in himself. I hope that the congregation didn't get lost en route. We sang, of course, Cowper's 'God moves in a mysterious way'.

The maps, young and ancient, slither on to the table. What dear, crumpled old friends. What shiny new friends, the latest of *Ashford and Romney Marsh*, Landranger 189, Ordnance Survey, with a view of Folkestone. There is the new *Cambridge Cycle Route Map*, Macpherson's *Fife, Kinross, Clackmannan and Perth* – last used by John Buchan? – and lovely maps with drawings of classy drivers and pipe-smoking walkers, and Bartholomew's *New Reduced Survey for Tourists*, one shilling. The magic when these are spread out, the endlessness of places!

A Platform Meditation

4th March

The unique melancholy of the unmanned railway station on a March afternoon. Just a big brother CCTV eye keeping watch. How long, how far, will we endure this secular version of God's unavoidable surveillance? However, the pleasant sadness of the grey platform and spanning iron bridge, the ghostly waiting-room, the framed timetables down which the rain slips. I have arrived with twenty minutes to spare as usual and there is nothing to do except think or not think, to meditate on BR or my life or, as usually happens, to allow the potency of train travel to seduce me. Somewhere in Proust's vast novel the narrator observes that there are place-names which one reads on railway stations, Vézèlay, Beauvais, etc., which turn an entire city into a cathedral, whereas the name Balbec, which he happens to read above the refreshment-room door, although that of a small seaside town, will in time extend for him personally to the size of a universe. Like Felixstowe, the old church and the new resort haven't all that much to say to each other. The first thing which the narrator does on leaving the station is to call on the carved apostles of old Balbec. As though pleased to be noticed once more, they 'were awaiting me as though to do me reverence. With their benign, blunt, mild faces and bowed shoulders they seemed to be advancing upon me with an air of welcome, singing the Alleluia of a fine day.'

At this moment I am simply waiting on a familiar Suffolk unmanned platform on a March afternoon and reduced to watching litter being blown into laurels and, although mind-less, it is also nice. Where else could I achieve such vacuity? The polished track ends in infinity in both directions. Then a few passengers arrive, some for the coast, some for the interior. They do not speak but stare discreetly at each other over the great divide. I examine the not quite dead plants which, unlike those in the parable, have taken root in the rock (concrete) and seeded themselves in other modest situations, groundsel, herb robert, a tiny flat mat of yellow corydalis not yet entirely trodden out of existence. A passenger turns his back on us to read the libels on their friends which school-children have written on a wall. Two seagulls arrive and treat us warily. My empty head now beginning to fill up with dreams etc. and, thinking of the apostles singing Alleluia to me on a fine day, I find myself on a teenage bike ride to look at churches, one after the other, and greeting wooden angels, looking up at them as they beat about the roof with their blue and red wings, and nodding to a Tractarian Lady here and there. And it was as Proust said, a polite return of greet-ings. Too soon now, for a pair of rattling carriages put a stop to platform meditation, I was on my way. I felt like a Desert Father being obliged to leave his bit of grit for some ravishing shrine which said nothing.

It is a wonderful gardening spring. How often can that be said? I work in jeans and jersey and the air is soft and sharp. At four the river of starlings flows over me. I am tidying up the rear of the old farmhouse whose cat-slide roof descends to within a few feet of the lawn. Many thousands of snow-drops are still at the white tip stage in the wood. I pull ivy from what remains of the farm wall and brush the huggermugger bricks, among which are some Roman tiles, presumably from the 1869 restoration of the church. This few yards of patched wall contains bricks of all ages and flints from the Stone Age. They cling to each other as mortar fails and purpose vanishes. Yet how handsome it remains, this free-standing wall come to light in Lent.

Cloud Kingdoms

5th March

I am a chronic cloud-watcher, a condition which may have started when I was reading one of those hold-all philosophies such as Lin Yutang's *The Importance of Living*. I would have been about fourteen and, no doubt, should it have been a holiday, mother would have been calling in vain to where I lay hidden in the tall grass. Errands. Not that they were always avoidable and put my more or less reasonable shape to vast walks and bike rides to fetch this or that. William Hazlitt and John Clare were self-confessed skivers. There they were, flat on their backs on the good earth, their eyes travelling along cirro-cumulus routes, their heads filled with vaporous wonders whilst the world shouted for them to do this or do that. This morning the white cat and I cloud-watched together as the sun came up. What Dolomites, what Snowdons, what golden gates. She closed her jade green eyes against the glitter. I cancelled all rational thought. And we might have remained like this until kingdom-come had not the kettle boiled. 'O ye Clouds, bless ye the Lord.'

In the village we splosh about, for it is O ye rains with a vengeance. The subtle drainage system which kept us all dry for centuries is lost under tarmac and new housing and we don't know where to find it. But then water did always lie about in March, so as to make mirrors for budding trees. I have mended my ways and purchased King Edward seed potatoes and set them out in trays to 'strike'. Last spring I allowed the kitchen garden to go wild. Oh the shame of it. This year it shall bear, shall flourish. Digging it over where generations of farmers (or most likely their wives) have dug it is a treat, the rich soil falling from the spade, the robin helping. Looking down now, not up. Christmas roses are in bloom by the wall, and we shall sing, 'Once in Royal David's City' on Mothering Sunday, this to my mind being the best mother-hymn we know.

Back at the desk, back to the window so as not to be distracted by the rainy glories of the skies, I write about walking along the shingle beach from Aldeburgh to Orford and paying the boatman sixpence to row me across the river, and this too in springtime, though long ago when tides were 'neap' (a tide which occurs during the first or last quarter of the moon when sun and moon are in balance with each other). People sometimes talk about the tide of human existence and all things being equal, etc. The spring clouds say 'Phoo' to this. Moisture-laden yet weightless, they float across my retina with a suggestion of land masses, of marvellous journeys and dark destinations. I imagine Christ being received by them out of my sight. In a plane it is earth's geography which is taken from our sight.

Fetching letters from where the postman leaves them in

a tumbledown shed, I send up a hundred rooks from an ivy-smothered ash. Their squawks drown out an harmonious bird orchestra. They whirl in all directions, black, crying, dreadfully upset. I beg their pardon. They wing away in a kind of furious diamond over Tom's farm, leaving behind the reasonable song of a thrush. Stephen arrives and we make our semi-amphibious way to the pub by the river. Travelling clouds race over its slow motion surface and are broken up by static swans. We hang our heads over the bridge and become dizzy with the conflict of reflection. John Constable would have stared up and down at this spot.

Jane Austen – and the Badger-slide

15th March

When I serve the vicar at Little Horkesley I kneel on the cracked tomb of one of Jane Austen's relatives, a Mrs Knight who married again and came our way. She comes into mind as the great costume extravaganzas are about to burst upon us. The novelist's little world will be filmically (and let us admit enjoyably) inflated to a degree which she would have found unrecognisable, and her countrywomen will wear dresses, ride in carriages and dwell in rooms which to them would have been beyond the dreams of avarice. Those who do not understand Jane Austen say that her stories are really about class and money, but they are really about virtue. It is hard to screen virtue. Mr Knightley has a claim to be English literature's most virtuous character. Should he, like Mr Darcy, take a swim in the film, and become just a visible man, what will happen to the plot? Jane Austen herself was resolutely segregated from the scandal of her fiction when she died. She was buried in Winchester Cathedral on 18th July 1817, her funeral taking place in the morning so as not to disturb the services. There is no mention of her trade on the stone, simply her dislike of 'enthusiasm in religion', or the Methodists. Like millions of viewers, I will be entertained by the gifted travesty of her intentions and go back to her pages, recalling what E. M. Forster once said, when he acknowledged 'the measure-less content when I drag one of these shy, proud books to the centre of my mind'.

My willows are greening and are filled with birds. Some are so ancient that they reel about and give little woody screams, and shed logs. 'Mind your head, we are coming down.' During March I can look right through them from the studio window and see Tom's reservoir with its flashing water-birds and smart edges. The three village churches are jewel-boxes, each containing its amused reflections, its particular brightness. The bells ring clearly, the grass is new. Lent and its contradictions are everywhere. On the one hand the grim desert, on the other the *Benedicite* with its catalogue of natural experiences, its thankfulness for everything. Lent is a time for taking stock, I say from the pulpit, not only from what surrounds us, but of ourselves, and I continue virtuously on the problems of not being quite well and not quite happy. And then about the loneliness of God when he walks in the garden in the cool of the evening, and there is no Man to chat to. As George Herbert and other writers told us, our sense of our non-fittedness to walk with God is a great problem for him, as well as for us. Another problem for those who have to preach on Lent in the same spring-filled building year after year is to give some idea of what desert aloneness can do to the soul. Everything is against it. 'The world, the flesh and Satan dwell / Around the path I tread', we sing and think of primroses.

I found a badger-slide. The badgers slide down a ditch on one side of the lane and scramble up the opposite bank, leaving behind the kind of worn dirt tracks which we as children achieved with our bottoms. Badgers (*Meles meles*) are alarmingly large and have vertical black and white stripes down their faces like Wimbledon fans. Sometimes I listen to their grumpy arguments at the back of the house.

Snow at Last

17th March

The vernal equinox and winter are paying a hurried visit. A gale hoots up the valley and howls above the crops. There is a battle between white and green as the snow arrives. Plovers confer on the low field. My mighty ash, son of Wagner's Ash of the World, gives off pistol shots from its defiant boughs. The snow whitens grass but turns tarmac to onyx. It is two-jersey time. And to think that we thought it would never happen – winter! A hare makes a dash for it. In the study, where work has to be done, the white cat has descended from the bookcase where she normally reigns and has bagged my cushion. What to do? Pull up a hard seat and know your place. The snow briefly decorates the study window then slides to oblivion. 'Nothing lasts save eternal change' ('The Coming of Spring' by Honorat de Bueil). Winter throws its cold glance into my room. Wonderfully handsome blackbirds appear below. I think of the snow-capped griffins aloft on a Suffolk church tower as they watch east, north, south and west, medieval meerkats who have kept the small town safe from Satanic invaders since 1460. Who forgets the snows of childhood? On the radio Sir Ranulph Fiennes is slowly melting from his trip to the Eiger.

We have just come back from the annual Readers' Day meeting at Cambridge, an admirable event created by Canon John Woods. Readers, indigenous as they often are to a parish, need to fly its boundary now and then and see and hear a bigger argument. On this occasion to take stock of themselves during some talks on 'Listening and Accessibility'. Writers are of course chronic listeners but not very accessible. So here we all are once more at Selwyn College taking a yearly look at each other's faces and being surprised by what lies beyond us. The chaplaincy of Cambridge United Football Team for example. The largeness of this task silenced us. Did we imagine that it would be a pep talk in the changing-room? Football is a country, an empire, a state. Stuart, its Baptist priest, revealed it to us, that spiritual, noisy, vast parish of his along the Newmarket Road.

We listened to the need to be conversational, something I tend to preach. When we think of scripture we are apt to believe that its many messages, laws and insights come to us as official statements, whereas they often reach us via ordinary talk or conversation. In the Bible there is preaching and there is talking and its great figures are heard doing both. Jesus is frequently recorded getting into conversation with someone, male or female. Once his critics tried to 'entangle him in his talk'. St Paul adored conversation and was forever telling his converts to converse. But it had to be 'elevated' talk. '*Our* conversation is in heaven.' He told young Timothy that a Christian should be recognised by his conversation, his love, his purity. 'Meditate and show the kind of young man you are by the way in which you *talk*.' I have heard old people on the meals-on-wheels round say that they would sometimes rather have a nice long talk than the food.

There is a statistic for most of the things we do in a lifetime, a third of it asleep, several years of it eating etc., but there is no figure for one of its most delightful activities – talking. Talking to each other can be a way of talking to God. In Cambridge a girl runs, while talking into her mobile, getting a word in.

Young Men along the Border

5th April

Long walks in blue weather. Hills, water, the firmament, the rising corn, all azure, their blueness mistily integrating so that I can see everything yet nothing as it usually is. One walk is to Tom's new reservoirs to watch the shelducks glide. The first has a kind of floating hedge of pussy palm, the sallow catkins which we, as children, took to church on Palm Sunday. Mallard scuttle from it, even their dark green heads touched with electric blue. As for the Suffolk bank of the Stour, it is Monet's blue palette range, spreading from murky to paradisal. A willow copse has burst its rabbit guards and dirty plastic writhes in the fresh nettles. Must return with a black bag. Must sow seeds; must mow. Must go to church most days. Must make time to do nothing in this turquoise scene. Just look. Scripture takes a medical interest in it. 'The blueness of a wound cleanseth away evil' – Proverbs 20.30. The hymns are agonising, often too tragic to sing. 'Can death thy bloom deflower?' Their physicality unavoidable. I think of the young Christ walking in springtime and the lake shining and its water-birds rising.

Another hike to the Hennys, great and small. They are high up and fairly Himalayan in our terms. It was here that Samuel Crossman wrote *A Young Man's Meditation* in 1664, having read in George Herbert that 'A Verse may find him who a Sermon flies'. One of Crossman's meditations was 'My song is love unknown'. Geoffrey Shaw took John Ireland out to lunch in a restaurant, pulled the poem out of his pocket and said, 'Can you set this?' Ireland read it, then set it on the back of the menu. There are two other Crossman poems with the same metre, should a present composer like to try his hand alongside John Ireland. One is about resurrection – 'I said sometimes with tears, Ah me! I'm loath to die!' Crossman was only in his twenties, well, and looking down at the Stour on a blue day.

The other poem is, naturally, 'Heaven':

> Earth's but a sorry Tent,
> Pitch'd for a few frail days,
> A short-leas'd Tenement;
> Heav'n's still my song, my praise.

He would spend his last two years on earth as Dean of Bristol with the horrors of the slave trade whirling around him. 'I come, my Lord! the floods here rise, these troubled Seas foam nought but mire . . .' I tramp along the narrow Henny lanes thinking of this youthful poet who had quite a rough time of it, ecclesiastically speaking, as he worked out his complex rhyming scheme. He once preached at St Mildred's in the Poultry on 'The Quiet Rest of God's Ark'.

When I was a boy, the Sudbury Boat Club always heaved its way along the river to Henny Swan, there to drink the local bitter and devour hot cross buns, and row its way home again, feeling pretty sick. Except for the Reach, as they called it, the Stour was in parts quite unreachable, with the locks fallen in and the pussy willows and every watery plant imaginable joining up to block its flow. In winter it flooded and could look like a miniature Mississippi, and was as blue as ice. It wound through the medieval common pastures on which, after Easter, the cattle would be turned out. They would stand stock still for a minute or two, unable to believe their luck, then gambol, romp, feed, cry a little. It was heaven.

The Concert Organist

9th April

David Kinsela and I make the golden journey, not to Samarkand, but to Wiston, the oil-seed rape having come into bloom. There it stretches, a yellow world from parish to parish, and above it by night a full yellow moon to return its stare. David has been recording Buxtehude's *Six Days of Creation* on the Aubertin organ at Saint-Louis-en-I'lle in Paris and the sumptuous music, like dark honey, has sweetened the ancient farmhouse rooms. But now we tread it out to the far river (two miles) and to the little Norman field church with its faded wallpaintings and vast chancel arch, its vault-like chill and, outside, its crisp sward. Another organist, Paul Taylor, killed in the Western Desert at twenty-four, has his name on the churchyard bench and I see him high up at the west end looking up the settings for the Easter Anthems. 'Christ our passover is sacrificed for us, therefore let us keep the feast.' Next to where Paul so briefly sat, there is a barrel organ and places for the singing-men. Outside in the afternoon sunshine the graves glow amidst the cow-parsley which will soon wonderfully overwhelm them. They are putting a little flock into George's paddock. This achieved, we have tea in the Hall, Fiona apologising for the hot kitchen, which amazes David. There is a moment at the end of his organ recitals when he aches for his native Australia, when he longs for Sydney and his dog, whose name I have forgotten. Back at Bottengoms Farm we listen to more Buxtehude on the Paris organ, to the fine hymn 'Lord Christ, God's only true Son'. David stretches and curls his thin fingers and says he has arthritis. So had Henry James, I tell him. All that handwriting, all this keyboard playing. Hands can only take so much. He glances at mine, knobbly from all that digging. Ah, flesh, ah cold and heat. Ah, lamb chops and new potatoes for dinner.

The guest gone, I work on my Kilvert lecture. I am back once more in 1870s Herefordshire where another walker feels the Easter weather, gathers primroses, hoes an old neighbour's garden for him, looks over the pulpit's ledge to see below him at Evensong some people who had heard his sermon at Matins in another church. Francis Kilvert was like Paul Taylor at Wiston, a young man whose duties in a country church would be brief. He died – peritonitis – when he came back from his honeymoon, and the floral arches to the rectory with which the village welcomed him would remain for his funeral. Yet is there a more vital, springtime-filled, healthier book than *Kilvert's Diary*? He wrote it, he said, to say that 'I was here', on the lovely earth in April. It is one of the best English country-books ever written and I long for everybody to read it – especially Anglicans. Kilvert did his duty as a curate and would lecture the young on Temptation. What a nerve. But how he adored being alive. How he *walked*. And how clear were his eyes, noting everything and everybody, and with a kind of bliss. You wonder why one of those Hay girls didn't snap him up. But then a curate on a hundred a year ... I once walked from Hay to Clyro, his parish, and I imagined that I faced his same clouds. The Black Mountain was behind me. I was staying at Bronith where he helped the old Waterloo soldier to hoe his crop and where his English-Christian voice chattered all the way saying, 'See this, don't miss that, and look, the light!'

Jenny Joseph

15th April

Two of the churches continue to be drenched in flower scent but Mount Bures, which is being decorated, smells nicely of paint. Nine coats, they say, on the ceiling. Easter doesn't go away. It hangs around in vestments and in the stained glass eyes and in the dusty shafts of sunshine, and the choir goes on munching what remains of the chocolate eggs. I entertain the poet Jenny Joseph ('When I am an old woman I shall wear purple') but in fact she arrives wearing the kind of motoring cap which a lady passenger would don if Mr Toad took her for a spin. There is always an interesting frisson when writers enter each other's dens for the first time and, quite properly, Jenny casts her eye around my bookish rooms as I bake the haddock and boil the spring greens and open the wine, for entertaining poets is a hungry business. Also it is odd for each of us to know one another so well in print and not at all out of it. I read her afresh when she has left, bumping up the track to Minchinhampton. Among other things she is an apologist for less than keen housekeeping, and is wry and witty. She celebrates selfishness, having earned it. The family having married, died etc., she says what many of us dare not say:

> When you are all away, my dears,
> The things will stay in place
> And oh, how nice to do things once
> Go out, and find when I come in
> A room has the same face.

I note that *Common Worship* has Exodus for Easter week Evening Prayer and the *Book of Common Prayer*, the Song of Solomon. Thus are our delights denied us. I read these amorous poems all through this morning, not allegorising them as instructed by the old moralists, but letting myself be ravished by these outpourings of the lover to his 'Shulamite' girl, and hers for him. It was the poetry which enchanted Richard Rolle and the Spanish mystics, and which Rolle called *The Fire of Love*, a favourite book of mine, written in Yorkshire in 1343:

> I ask you, Lord Jesus,
> to develop in me, your lover,
> an immeasurable urge towards you,
> an affection that is unbounded,
> a longing that is unrestrained,
> a fervour that throws discretion to the winds!

'Would a Rambling Rector rose thrive on her tall north wall?' Jenny Joseph had enquired somewhat anxiously. It might. Rambling Rectors should twist and turn in all directions. I plant potatoes, dibbling them in, keeping the rows straight. The birds nest all around, sweetly calling and making it plain that they will be glad to see the back of me. Low Sunday approaches, *Dominican in Albis* when the newly baptised hung up their white robes. Sundays were neither High nor Low to Richard Rolle, being perpetually in love, as he was. 'To love and be loved is the delightful purpose of God to all mankind.'

Ben and the Marmalade Cat

18th April

B en and his parents arrive. What will he have? 'Black tea.'
I wave a tea-bag around in scalding water, he sips and
says, 'Urgh!' He is nine and he virtuously declines crisps.
I assure him that I am impervious to foody-ism and that I
won't mind if he turns to a skeleton before my very eyes. His
parents cry, 'Ben, Ben . . .' Can he watch *Dr Who*? We with-
draw to a silent room. It is a June in April night and the
scent of late primroses enters the wide window. Once the
programme is over Ben will re-enact his little ritual, his holy
visitation to the *Orlando* books on the bottom shelf, now
'slightly foxed' by some five years' administration of his small
hands. *Orlando Buys a Farm, Orlando Becomes a Doctor . . .*
what will it be? We knew Kathleen Hale. On account of
these volumes she was 'Moggie' to us and some of us are
transmogrified in her gorgeous lithographs. I would gladly
have given these books to Ben but it would have broken a
condition. When I was his age a cobble-stone had to remain
in the centre of a brick courtyard and be ritually touched by
me once a day. Ditto an iron ring on a horse-post had to be
jingled whenever I went that way. However, having ordered
black tea, Ben continues in his new sophistication by asking,
'May I borrow this *Orlando*?' And I play my part in the ritual
by replying. 'Of course!' and adding unnecessarily, 'But take
good care of it.' These stories which are his, really, have to
stay here with me.

All three churches are heavy with Easter flowers. They are

gothic pomanders, their fine carved skins stuck with scents. Low Sunday for High church but Shepherd Sunday for the likes of us, Emmaus and *Agnes Dei* time. And the heat of the sun! Looking around the churchyard I see a stone to a man christened 'Golden'. That would have given pause at the font. Disgraceful font tales come to my ragbag mind, like that in *Kilvert's Diary*. Mr Moule, the Vicar of Fordington – his son Horace taught Thomas Hardy classics as they walked through the fields – told Kilvert about a predecessor of his. 'One day there was a christening and no water in the Font. "Water, Sir!" said the clerk in astonishment. "The last parson never used no water. He spit in his hand."'

A pause here while I read some *Orlando the Marmalade Cat* and think of Moggie with her fringe and her wit, and who departed *this* life at a hundred and one. Her cat Orlando was the onlie begotten of these masterpieces and he only made twenty-three. One day, when God has put me down, then lifted me up, Ben will arrive to claim his own and the ritual will be snapped. My white cat has been much infested by dogs of late. They run ahead of their owners and noisily lap up her leavings, swiping the furniture with their tails, and given much to ecstasy. She takes to the high ground, an apple-tree, the top shelf. David's spaniels cry outside like those not fit for paradise, having swum in the reservoir and too soaking to be let in. How they mourn! 'Be good!' he hollers. If only we could be, just good, eating what is set before us, not bending our books, not shopping *all* the time. It is St Mark's time. No hanging around with Mark. He is young and swift, the Ezekiel of the New Testament. He said, 'A spirit lifted me and carried me along, and I went full of exaltation, the hand of the Lord strong upon me.' Mark too went at a tremendous pace. With him joy hurries to displace fright and loss. He could write with brevity and great beauty.

David and the Oxlips Wood

23rd April

Hawthorns are snow slopes of flowers, ditches vanish under growth, in some 'neglected' churchyards the dead are canopied with cow parsley, a plant of lace and moonlight, as Geoffrey Grigson called it. Forty of us attend the bluebell party at Tiger Hill, ourselves as seasonal as these acres of wild hyacinth which have watched us grow up, grow old. Although it is early afternoon, nightingales entertain us with a kind of part-song, a string of notes here, a throaty burst there. It is hot where it is usually chilly, Mediterranean almost. We are in a medieval warren and a Victorian brickyard, a wildwood and a badger land. I have come straight from Matins where, unseasonally, I have preached on Benedict and his Rule, and we have sung Jean de Santeul's 'Disposer supreme, and Judge of the earth', with the sun pouring in on us. The bluebell picnic friends struggle to their feet and straggle off into the Tiger Hill wilds. The paths of crushed petals echo with ex-clamations, but not with that tragic cry of 'AI, AI' which came from the suffering of Hyacinthus, accidentally killed by Zephyrus during a game of quoits. Apollo resurrected Hyacinthus as a flower, but not as *our* flower, the white stalks of which make a slippery standing, and the scent of which takes us back to bicycle days when, laden so much with bluebells for mother, we could hardly pedal.

David had arrived the day before, minus the dogs and with the look of a man with an expedition in his head. He has looked forward to showing me 'his' oxlips for ages. The ownership is a just one. He is one of Nature's pilgrims and his walks are like sacred visitations. He introduces me to his finds with excitement and pride. Now off we go to Bull's Wood in Cockfield – where Robert Louis Stevenson used to stay with his uncle, the rector. This wood was first written down in 1267 says the Suffolk Wildlife's Trust board at its entrance. At first, all that I can read into it is the blue present, with the rape fields lying around it like old gold rugs and the silent farm down the track burning in the windy heat, and there is that mysterious quiet which forests impose on their intruders.

David's eagerness to watch my first sight of his oxlips soon fades. He has brought me on a wild oxlip chase. As if to pacify him, a nice clump of oxlips stands in our path. Thankfully, he kneels before it, delicately threading the yellow bells through his brown fingers, turning them like raised tower-bells for me to look into them. Quoting Richard Mabey now, oxlips (*Primula elatior*) survive in a triangle of land on the boulder clay between Stansted in Essex and Bury St Edmunds and Stowmarket in Suffolk, and here we are, just there. 'But,' says David, 'there should have been a great spread of them, not these few! It is this July in April what has done it, upset all the flower clocks!' Penetrating the ancient wood we find more oxlips amongst the coppicing, more than enough to thrill to. Purple orchis as well. Not much birdsong but winds too light to blow quoits about. And ever-present this antiquity, these woodland paths trodden by villagers who went to mass and who spoke 'Chaucer', and who were sexy in Maytime and who did well to last until they were forty. They didn't think much of oxlips, being not one thing or the other, a primrose or a cowslip.

The Horses on the Hill

25th April

'No house should be *on* any hill or on anything', wrote Frank Lloyd Wright in his *An Autobiography*. 'It should be *of* the hill, belonging to it, so hill and house could live together each the happier for the other.' Bottengoms Farm is roughly contemporary with a book called *De Magnete*, written just up the road by William Gilbert in 1600 in which the terms 'electric attraction', 'electric force' and 'magnetic pole' were first to appear in the English language. Thus I see an author in his study and a farmer down by the river toiling away, the one letting in the light, the other keeping out the weather. 'Electric' is Greek for 'amber' which, when rubbed on the warm arm, sends a current through the conducting flesh. However, several centuries would pass before it illuminated my shadowy rooms. The old friends who inhabited them in my youth sadly put away the Aladdin oil lamps with their battered parchment shades and had a single bulb hung from a beam in each room, never loving this improvement. A generator in the garden linked up with Duncan's farm over the hill and the light would quiver when he switched on his grain-drier. 'There', they would complain, 'you never got that with the lamps!' Brought up as a child in subdued interiors, I still do not possess a torch and am an expert on the degrees of darkness, of which there are many.

The unknown house-builder set his farm due east. As everyone knew, death and sickness dwelt in the south. Summer poisoned the ponds, bred disease. Thus I am facing bright dawn all the year round. The new sun rolls along the hill like a hot penny 'fading the furniture' as they used to complain, not to mention the front door, over which a roll of beach canvas would be let down to prevent the paint from bubbling. Brown or green paint it would have been, not my Trafalgar Blue.

The commotion of the Easter services over, I am able to think at last. Morning tea, morning light, morning cat, and the roll-penny sun hill – 'enough to blind you'. Or enlighten you. The hill mourns the pony which has been put down. He was thirty-six. The children rode him. Oh, sorrow, sorrow. Oh mortality. Oh hill of horses, some ploughing, some idling, some gathering for a horse chat, with my sunshine on their backs. How do horses grieve? One of the many meanings of 'put down' is to dethrone. The small pony was dethroned from his high hill, as we shall be, bodily speaking. But bees are about, bending the sloe blossom to their will. I sit in an old wooden chair which I have mended at great cost and drink tea, and give praises to God for the lawnmower, and for being due east, and for still being enthroned of a sort. Seabirds, sniffing turned earth, whizz by. How well we sung the Easter Anthems. How patient I was this year when we came to the dreadful 'That were a *present* far too small' and not remotely murderous. How good I am this daybreak, facing up to things. I make a silent resolution where the hill is concerned. I will climb it and see what is going on all around it. I will give the stricken beasts a consolitary word and they will give me a cautious look through the electric fence. Their paradise is guarded by fiery currents. They will pity me for having to feed so low down, for dwelling in the vortex of the rape ocean. They think I have come up for air, but I have climbed the hill to give them the time of day.

The Eloquent Border

27th April

To the west: Housman's coloured counties are mostly coloured rape-yellow but dove-grey skies and huge distances act to modify their brief harshness. I am paying my bi-annual respects to that Anglican holy land known as the Welsh Border where George Herbert, Henry Vaughan. Thomas Traherne and Francis Kilvert, in turn, appeared like eloquent stars, quite how or why we will never know. First to Hereford to talk about the Curate of Clyro, as William Plomer, his excellent editor, called him. After great grousing on my part the complete *Diary*, unseen for ages, is back in print. Editors so often being ignored or abused, I pay rightful homage to William Plomer for his perfect dealings with Kilvert who once wrote, 'Why do I keep this voluminous journal? I can hardly tell. Partly because life appears to me such a curious and wonderful thing that it almost seems a pity that such a humble and uneventful life as mine should altogether pass away without some such record as this . . .' He had returned from one of his long walks. It was the autumn of 1874 and he was thirty-three. The walk had been filled with Border sounds, the belling of a buck, the fluttering of a coot, the cry of swans, the clicking of the reels of a pair of fishermen by the stream, the soft murmur of falling leaves, 'the merry voices of the Marquis's children at play'. The following day Kilvert gave a lecture on the News. It was in the school and everyone listened to him describe the funeral of Dr Livingstone, the visit of the Czar, shipwrecks, bombings, the usual things. I remember my father telling me how the schoolmaster in his Suffolk village would read *The Times* aloud to a crowd of unlettered folk, in the playground if fine, in the classroom if wet – this every Saturday morning. We, the Kilvert Society, listened to that long ago young voice in the Bishop's Palace.

In the Cathedral Traherne had just been honoured with a pair of glowing windows which prismatically reflected those life-appreciating words from his *Centuries* which begin. 'The Corn was Orient and Immortal Wheat, which never should be reaped.' He also told us that 'Love is the true means by which the world is enjoyed. Our love to others and others' love to us. We ought therefore above all things to get acquainted with love, for love is the root and foundation of Nature.' Most of us have come to Traherne via the inspired introduction of the Reverend Richard Birt, a local priest who for many years now has led us to Credenhill and its astonishing Christian informer. Henry Vaughan, a medical doctor from Llansantffread further along the Border, had a way of beginning a great poem conversationally – 'I saw Eternity the other night' or 'They are all gone into the world of light' – before hurrying the reader into a metaphysical glory. George Herbert of course was no more than a little child at Newport. 'Change at Newport' say the trains. He was always on his way, sometimes with his Christ, often he thought ahead of him. Either he or his Lord were in a process of catching up. 'I struck the board, and cried, "No more: I will abroad."' A Welshman in Wiltshire.

My friends put on a little concert in their barn, a consort of viols plays melancholy delights by Bull and Purcell. Earlier we had walked in the hills accompanied by a German sheep-dog who apologised for looking like the Hound of the Basker-villes and whose joy was infectious. I thought of Francis Kilvert 'villaging' as he called it, stepping into hovels – and into thrilling situations.

My Workroom

30th April

I write each day with my back to the landscape, and especially these last few days because it has been extra distracting. The steep untypical East Anglian hill with its present April growth and its past hint of pre-history is usually diverting enough, but this week it has been given the Marc Chagall touch in the form of some escaped black pheasants and a freed black rabbit. Do not look out. Looking inwards I see what I have seen for decades as I settle to the firm Victorian writing-table, first to have a brief priming the pump little read, this morning it was Augustus Hare's *Biographical Sketches*, and then to write for three hours. The room is ancient beyond telling and was where the artist Christine Külenthal slept before it became my study. It is a house without corridors, a run-through where one passed in and out of private happenings without seeing them, such as Christine powdering her face by lamplight. Dead these thirty years, her simple make-up occasionally makes its presence known as I tread the wide floorboards from which not all the art of Dyson can draw the final dust.

Writers and artists are happiest when in their workrooms. Two journeys hang upon the walls of mine. One is taken by a sailing ship and the other by farm carts. The ship is an etching by Francis Unwin and the carts are a pencil drawing by his friend John Nash. Off they go, to the China Seas, to manure the fields. Books crowd around, all the poetry nearest to me. With my glasses on I can make out Betjeman, Blake, Browning, Byron, and through a haze many Lives. The big German press in which Christine kept her shoes now holds my manuscripts. Her forty pairs to my three pairs. Behind me and to hand is the holy bookcase, the three different hymnals for the three different village churches, the *Churchyards Handbook* – very exciting – some of the Prayer Books from Edward VI on, Julian, Rolle, Bunyan, Augustine, Sir Thomas Browne, all the latest things. And Helen Gardner's *Faber Book of Religious Verse* and, naturally, *The Holy Grail: Its Origins, Secrets and Meaning Revealed* by Malcolm Godwin, for I must keep up.

Time evaporates here. Farmers' children, four in a bed, or shepherds snoring, or a young man packing his bag for Waterloo or Gallipoli, or Biggin Hill, or the tall Slade girl putting on her Dorelia John dress in the dark and scattering her powder into the floorboards, and now myself, tapping and scribbling, careful not to look out for fear of seduction by the lovely day which lies the other side of the pane, or by some wicked author who is bent on catching my eye from his shelf. It is the feast of St Mark, that 'Stay awake!' saint, that swift mover of words, that thrilling activist. Old Paul, having run the race, and who is unutterably weary, longs for Mark's quickness. He tells Timothy, 'Pick up Mark and bring him with you . . . when you come, bring the cloak I left with Carpus, and the books, above all my notebooks.' In his 'The Eve of Saint Mark', John Keats seems to be looking from my study:

> And, on the western window panes,
> The chilly sunset faintly told
> Of unmatured vallies cold . . .

Except of course it is the chilly sunrise faintly told through an eastern window-pane. So he was a night writer in some small room where his habitation would be brief.

The Marvellous Story of Job

2nd May

Getting into Stansted was no trouble at all, it is the getting out which will be a trial. Thus Joachim arrives from Berlin on the dot of 9 p.m. The heat of the day lingers in the orchard. There is a noticeable growing darkness. It is the evening of the Sabbath. He does what he always does, collects the two brass candlesticks from the piano, searches around for a spotless napkin, takes the little Victorian christening cup (whose?) from the sideboard, places two bread rolls in the linen and crunches them up, puts wine in the cup, opens the napkin and sprinkles salt on the broken bread, gives us a sip and some crumbs, and begins. He says the 145th psalm in Hebrew. 'As for me, I will be talking of thy worship, thy glory, thy praise, and wondrous works, so that men shall speak of the might of thy marvellous acts . . .' And I think of them all standing there in the upper room. Night has come during this short service. The vine on the south wall rustles with sleeping birds. It is almost chilly and a barn owl rushes from a tree.

I am re-telling some Bible stories by way of sermons – this Sunday, Job. I do not present a contemporary equivalent, some high flyer with a glamorous wife brought low by a financial crash and Aids, for I now find myself shrinking from this usage of scripture. Job is a poem about the perennial problem of undeserved suffering. The wise entry in the *Oxford Dictionary of the Christian Church* says, 'Owing to the universal nature of the subject matter of the book' its age is of little importance, but maybe it was written about 400 BC. But how one would love to know the author: What kind of man, pen in hand, would have begun. 'There was a man in the land of Uz, whose name was Job, and that man was perfect and upright . . .' And then would have put this paragon through the mill before restoring him to his original grandeur or, rather, allowing God to give him twice as much as he had before, plus a lifespan of 140 years? The poem itself is mightily conceived – forty-two chapters. It contains some of the *Book of Common Prayer*'s most famous lines for funerals, and some of the most enduring platitudes for misfortune. These, of course, are spoken by Job's Comforters, the kind of people who hang over us in our hospital beds, or when a lover deserts us, or when we run into bankruptcy. But now I am doing what I said I would not do, updating the story for the pulpit. I must let the universal nature of the subject matter stay in its first form where its relevance to the human calamity at any time cannot be avoided, although I cannot help thinking that Job's wife and daughters are horribly similar to some of the women we meet in the Sunday papers. They are absolutely furious with him for ruining them. 'Curse God and die', says the wife. He tells her that she is a fool.

It is immediately after this domestic spat that the Comforters arrive – 'they had made an appointment to come to mourn with him and to comfort him'. Comforters always arrive by appointment, of course. To give these three their due they do not speak for a week – but *then*! The poet of Job is wonderfully witty. He allows the three Comforters a beautiful language which is useless, if that is not a contradiction. The poor sick man listens to lovely words. They awaken his soul, as it were, and he responds in some of the most remarkable self-confessing language to be found in literature. From wishing that he had not been born, Job tells us what it is like to be alive.

How Tiger Hill Began

7th May

The Bluebell Party at Tiger Hill looms large in our calendar and guests come from far and wide. That is, from Colchester to Cambridge. In 1917 a young woman doctor, Grace Griffith, arrived at the Sanatorium nearby, an icy palatial building crowded with sick children, sick soldiers, perishing landworkers, to find a hide-out for her scanty leisure hours in a bluebell and nightingale wood. Immensely kind – and immensely formidable – Dr Grace gradually took in some fifty acres of what originally had been a scrap of the old wildwood of England. Once upon a time its name was Blakean, Tyger Hill. Once it was a medieval warren, once a Victorian Brickworks. Now it is our most loved nature reserve. Once, when we were boys and girls, we gathered for no reason other than they spread before us in illimitable profusion, such quantities of bluebells to tie on to our bikes that it became difficult to mount them. Sad trails of them along the stony lane were evidence of our floral rape. Now we teeter along thin muddy tracks between the psychedelic blueness, stopping now and then to hear the nightingales.

Four this year. They are near yet at the same time distant, overhead yet remote. Small unassuming birds with broad chestnut tails to whom only great poets can sing back, John Keats and John Clare. Keats's song was one of tragic farewell, Clare's that of a boy naturalist. Steadying myself on the slippery, crushed bluebell stems, I listened to the deep cover music. One of my bird books calls the nightingale's behaviour skulking and solitary, but I find it that of a creature who is beyond our mere spying and observation, one that is born for our ears, not our eyes. Its song is loud and grand, and in glorious sequence. '*Wheeeet, tac tue, kerrr, chook-chook-chook, piu, piu, piu*', this last movement almost too ravishing to describe.

As unseen this Sunday afternoon moment are Tiger Hill's badgers, rabbits, dormice, shrews, bats, toads, frogs, newts, grass snakes, lizards, slowworms, woodpeckers and owls. But we, the listening human pack, are like people turned to stone by birdsong. The soft spring rain falls across us. The nightingales may be in hiding but we can almost watch the trees grow. I think of Dr Grace with her faint drawl of a voice, the saviour of these ancient acres. If we are to have authority in the countryside, let it be like hers. She was a Christian Socialist who knew – as well as nightingales and bluebells – Percy Dearmer, Clutton Brock, the Webbs and William Temple, Millicent Fawcett and Maude Royden. She toiled without complaint eighty hours a week for £250 a year. 'Please, Dr Grace, may we pick the bluebells?' 'Of course, of course, dear ones.'

Driving home via the Stone Age settlement by Smallbridge, we heard a tyre go flap-flap-flap. Mercifully Doug Saunders, exercising his neighbour's dog, was passing by to help change the wheel. The pierced tyre revealed a violent slash, V-shaped and somehow shocking – something more than a puncture, more a mortal blow. We had run over a razor-sharp Stone Age artefact, a flint knife or weapon. Five thousand years had passed since it had been created and its time had come. It had cut our thick rubber and let out its wind. It had ravelled up Time, as Shakespeare would have said. The May rain had given it an extra shine and its owner would have been proud of it. The wetlands by the Stour were ridged with potatoes and sparkling with stones. Here was a flat tyre to elevate thought.

The Launch of the John Nash

13th May

Biblical rains for Rogation and for the launching of the *John Nash*, a multi-modal river punt. At first the downpour is playful, merely drenching us, but then the heavens tip it out and the willows thrash the surface of the Stour and the millrace makes white water. No organist at Mount Bures so we sing sweetly unaccompanied. The rain is no more than a dark threat at this moment. Rogation, *rogare*, ask. Ask, beg God not to flatten the May crops it would have been long ago. But who now worries about what goes on in the fields these days? Who in the village actually sees a field? Who looks at one? The birds of course, and I at this moment take them in as they threaten to become lakes. Dutifully with bowed

heads we ask for nothing for ourselves, only that it may soon
rain in Australia, that a lost child will be found, that the tent
by the river won't blow across into Suffolk. As John Keble
said – is not his College our patron? –

> The former and the latter rain,
> The summer sun and air,
> The green ear, and the golden grain,
> All thine, are ours by prayer.

How can my Rogation sermons cease being farming history, I ask myself? Is there a soul present with 'dearth' or
'plenty' on his mind? Yet the childlike persistence of this
annual asking is at least a reminder of the Fatherhood of
God. We snuff the altar candles, count the offering, seize our
umbrellas and make for the *John Nash* where a lovely dark
girl, who looks like a figure from an Etruscan frieze come to
life, waits to pour a glass of champagne on its hull. In 1929 a
young artist and his wife punted here during the August
holidays, she lying back on cushions, he in his gaudy pyjamas
poling their boat out of the reeds. I had shown the Box
Brownie snaps of this idyll to Francis, with today's result, the
multi-modal river punt awaiting its maiden voyage. The rain
at this moment was no more than a pelting of coin-size drops.
Would the young boat-builders finish their casual account of
how they created this enchanting craft before we were all
swept away by the torrent above?

But then, braving this, the *John Nash* was manned and
passengered, unlooped and oared, steered and on its way.
Wormingford millpool spread before it, as it had done for
the artist perched on his decidedly non-multi-modal vessel.

He had come here via the Western Front, from the roar of Ypres to the crashing of this little stream on the banks of which both Tom Gainsborough and John Constable had set their sights. And within walking distance of each other. During our long friendship I rarely heard John Nash refer to either of them. It puzzled me during my youth. Only gradually did I witness what he saw, the day-new river, the flashing of it, the immediacy of its climate, the pike stirring, the roach darting under the bridge. I would lie reading as he sketched, each of us lost for entire afternoons in some dateless present. And then his, 'Call it a day, old fellow!' But what day? And then gradually and in the nature of things, the vanishing and just the Stour flowing.

Lunch in the barn to 'Brittonic music by Twm Twm'. I quote. Wild stuff. And even wilder music as the rain proper, no longer restrained to mere drenchings, unleashes its possibilities. Will the cars and the multi-modal punt join forces and sail out to Harwich?

The Fairweather Visitors

15th May

Mid-May. I beg Paul the woodman to cut down an ancient willow which is doing breaking and entry. Now on its last legs, it is having a last sprawl. Should I wake during the small hours, and there is a faint breeze, I listen to it softly scraping against the window like a tree-Heathcliff begging to come in. Vast willows put on a spur when they are falling to bits. Paul's felling tools drone a dirge all afternoon.

Richard Mabey arrives and we do our nightingale and bluebell stint. The day is dull and still. A kingfisher skims below the bridge which links Essex with Suffolk. The river is aquamarine and strong-flowing. We talk of Edward Thomas getting his glut of England before Flanders when 'a bullet stopped his song'. We have no idea what has stopped the Tiger Hill nightingales' song, but silent they are. But there are a million compensations, scurrying deer and handsome colonies of yellow archangel, the most we have ever seen, all along the stream. 'Why were dead nettles, deaf nettles, dumb nettles, named *archangelus* in the Middle Ages, unless from the angelic quality (which is hardly archangelic) of not stinging?' asked Geoffrey Grigson. And there, on the far side of the stream is the Long Acre. I think of the long acres in my life, the one which we reached halfway to grandmother's, the one which stretched behind my house at Debach, and the one I have explored in London and which would have been mowed (long acres appeared to have been more stately meadow than field) where the monks of Westminster would have walked, especially during Ascension-tide, their habits trailing in the rich spring grass. The great poet William Langland took his name from his mother's long acre, a flat strip of earth under the Herefordshire Beacon. The Lord left this world at its most transcendant moment, when it was at its natural best. Were the Middle Eastern swallows winging it to Britain?

Fairweather visitors of another kind are on the wing, or more accurately on the A12. 'We thought we would come and see you. Don't do anything. We'll bring a picnic. What is the track like?' The answer to the last is, 'Like a long, twisting and waving corridor of flowers. Like a living wall. Like nothing you will see this side of paradise. Call it cow parsley in excelsis. Only mind the bend where the telephone pole totters, not to mention the weary jogger. On Saturday nights the village hall bursts with learning as the Quiz tables are set up, or throbs with line-dancing, as we all make our escape from television. Not a visible stroke of work is done on the land. On the contracted-out farm it is like perpetual sabbath. Stillness mounts on stillness as weedless crops drink greedily from the sprayers. There is a lot of supermarket veg growing in immaculate rows, as is only right.

An in-any-weather visitor is Meredith. He is the quiet countryman who carries his reserve to the limit. Long ago I said something like, 'Meredith – a Welsh name?' and naturally received no answer. When the novelist Ronald Firbank was asked a direct question he would say, 'I wonder'. But Meredith was silent. He reminded me of Uncle Bill whose eyes were forerunners of my own and into which he would stare impersonally, as one might into the eyes of a portrait. We would sit opposite each other by the coal fire and let it do the talking. Meredith does jobs for me now and then. 'How are you, Meredith?' We are together, wordy me, wordless him.

At St Mawes

17th May

Cornwall again. Only after many a summer, so that the voices which once welcomed me, Charles Causley's and James Turner's, are now only to be heard in their books. The King Harry Ferry cranks us over the river and there is St Mawes, bridal white and waiting. Yachts dance on Carrick Roads. There are flurries of May rain and bright statements of May sun, and the profound peace which says that a party will soon begin. Though not for a while, not before we get our Cornish landings. Not indeed before we are home again in Wormingford with the pollen of Alexanders (*Smyrnium olusatrum*) still dusting the car. So we explore what I once knew so well and haven't seen for ages and are half lost at times in the narrow green canyons which penetrate the rock, looking for old addresses, visiting John Betjeman in his grave, hearing the yelling gulls, myself coming to roost in what used to be part of my annual territory. There is the garden gate at Treneague through which is the garden I weeded. There are the signposts with the Thomas Hardy references, Lanivet, Tresparret, which we never failed to quote. There on the Lizard is the very pub where we wrote a tale, only now it has a new name. At night we join the rollicking locals for fish and chips. They are like the staff of some great house before the guests arrive from town, noisy Beryl Cook models all roaring away.

Back home they will be bracing up for the Flower Festival. Could we hide in Cornwall until it is all over? What a wicked

thought. How would the Quota be paid if everyone entertained such notions? Holidays play havoc with our duties. I
tell my friends that we may as well stay in St Mawes for ever,
just looking out the window at the violet water and the
slender figure in the wetsuit skimming across it. At Daymer
Bay bulging pillow-shaped kites tug surfers over the sea at
twenty miles an hour. In St Enodoc Golf Club, where we are
hospitably permitted to lunch, a kind of Arthurian round
table is full of talk – boastings maybe. In St Enodoc's church
we sit and recall Betjeman's wild funeral, the coffin buffeted
by the gale, the long line of mourners struggling to stay
upright, the sand giving way at every step. It wasn't an easy
journey at the happiest of times. In 'Sunday Afternoon Service
is St Enodoc's Church, Cornwall' it was:

> Come on! come on! This hillock hides the spire,
> . . . These shivering stalks of bent-grass, lucky plant,
> Have better chance than I to last the storm,
> Oh kindly slate of these unaltered cliffs,
> Firm, barren substrate of our windy fields!

But little or no wind for us. It is April in May, with bursts
of June, a topsy-turvy climate. The wild flowers are a sight.
The walls are called hedges. Rivulets run unseen. Bays appear
where you believe you are inland. Cadgwith is thatched
throughout and the fishing boats are all blue and waiting for a
Newlyn School painter to do them, ignorant of time's passage.
Lizard Point is a desiccated ending. Tall valerian, *Centranthus
ruber*, or if you prefer, 'drunkards', rides every bank, waving
tipsily as we pass. The non-smoking rules must be ruining
the serpentine ashtray trade. I think of all those immigrant

priests who sailed in with their tale of a beautiful young God who was defiled and killed, who rose from the netherworld out of sheer love and put a stop to death. No wonder they were more sanctus than reverend. St Mawes, says our map, St Teath, St Just in Roseland.

The Passion of St Edmund

21st May

The may is browning, the rape rotting. A cuckoo and a nightingale at Tiger Hill sing at once. And it rains for the first time since March. I hear it coursing through the guttering and see it writhing through the weeds on the track. How can I praise it, with what words? The white cat lets it thunder around her where she muses below a shrub. A daft weatherman on the radio apologises for 'a miserable day'. I allow it to soak me as I put the finishing touches to the tubs of sweetpea seedlings, with their tall cane wigwams. The once pallid earth darkens under the onslaught and buds open before my very eyes. Or almost.

We attend the Historical Society to listen to a lecture on Edmund, our local saint. The car-park is packed. Who would have believed that he would have been such a draw? But it turns out that although we have a respectable audience it is the footballers who have swelled the spaces. Distantly, they run and shout by the Stour, leap and hug and holler, just like on the telly. The village hall curtains are drawn and the family tree of the Suffolk royal family glimmers on the screen. What a multitude of branches and tendrils there are as brief life follows brief life. These are the Wuffings from Sweden and Sutton Hoo, and the lecturer says that they can trace themselves back to nourishing wolves like the Roman emperors. Who was it that protected the decapitated head of the martyred King Edmund, but a wolf. This creature lurks under a miserere seat here and there, so watch out.

As we are in Bures we require learned confirmation that Edmund was crowned above our river, as our grandparents maintained, but the lecturer is not so sure. What is certain is that the poor young man, so brave, so holy, had to become the St Sebastian of England. When the lecturer showed his university students a medieval painting of this execution, with all the arrows in a vertical row, they cried, 'One hundred and thirty-six!' Maybe Edmund would have had a go at darts. Such frivolity over, we enter via the doubly illuminated manuscripts into his glory. The loop in the Stour would have been the same, the spring rains, the playful young men, the remorseless cruelties on the News, the churches with their talk of love, the ravens darkening the sky, the boats bobbing in the reeds. The captured King re-enacted the captured Christ. In *The Passion of St Edmund* the Dane says, 'Know you not that I have power to kill you?' and the King retorts in 'a weak but firm reply', 'Know you not that I know how to die?' And so it goes on, the idiot fighting, through the ages.

It is Rogation but, having so much, including this rain, what more dare we ask of God? At Little Horkesley Henry the vicar takes a procession through the rape and onions and corn, and we salve the asking question by asking for others.

The fields are wet, the air sweet and soggy. The Cross flashes like Edmund's spurs as he hid under Hoxne bridge, giving him away. It sways past lilacs and laburnums and eventually under the churchyard limes. The gravestones sparkle like jewels. Late rains have laid the human dust, put it to rest. St Edmund's was shut up in a gold box for centuries. Now and then they opened it, to music, and peered inside to see that it hadn't blown away. It was a cure-all for body and soul. I hope that there were days by the river when he could forget all this. Just lie in the wet grass without his crown and listen to Suffolk birds.

The Fate of the Imagination

22nd May

It is a late May afternoon and I am engaged in that form of meditation known as weeding. How the May birds sing! I am on my knees hoicking out the undesirables with a nice new silver fork, untwirling the everlasting sweetpea fronds from a nettle and sadly, for they always make me think of that Dürer drawing, piling up the dandelions. I cut fresh edges and smell pear blossom. A lean tomcat calls to pay court to Kitty, who eyes him sanguinely, safe in the knowledge that there is nothing doing. The sun is warm, the grass wet, the jeans muddy. It is great to be alive. 'Oh, the work, the work!' laments a caller. I think of Gilbert White peering from the rectory window at 'my weeding women' and most likely not believing that they could be at their prayers.

My meditations are random and ranging. For instance I contemplate St James, the man from Bethsaida, which means the House of Fish (just as Bethlehem means the House of Bread) swimming away to Compostela in his silver box, and what a welcome he got! In her pilgrimage book *On Glory Roads*, Eleanor Munro says that 'It is the fate of the imagination sometimes to be trapped in the very structures it invents . . . the Lord, as a construct of thought, understood this natural condition. He who had been a wayfarer, coming out of the dark like a wind, standing over Sinai like a flame, travelling north in the Ark, in scriptural fact approached his installation in a Temple with a troubled mind. "Down to this day I have never dwelt in a house . . . I made my journey in a tent and a tabernacle . . . Did I ever ask any of the judges why they had not built me a house of cedar?" (2 Samuel 7.5–9).'

All I can think of as I dig away is that nobody requires a house in Maytime. A mighty stand of cow-parsley three feet tall below the kitchen window, almost in flower, dares me to touch it and so like some petty deity I let it live. I will watch it whiten and sway as I wash up, and become a lovely fragment of that glorious transformation of the English roads, their ravishing take-over by *Anthriscus sylvestris* in a week or two's time. I always cut tall stems of it to place in big old pots by the brick bread oven so that I can enjoy it inside and out, and where it kindly makes its own starry, branchy perfect shape. This would have been anathema to the men who built the oven for whom it was 'Devil's meat'. They should have got out more and into that divine universe of flowers.

Late that evening I watch Muriel Spark seeking to define her art in slowly accurate sentences, the Scottish rawness attractively present. So broke was she in London that a stationer had to give her the five quarto sheets on which to write her debut story 'The Seraph and the Zambezi'. She has always written with a ballpoint pen, three to each novel. I wrote my first books with a relief nib, dipping and sliding it along the ruled foolscap, but these days it is three to a card ballpoints. Recently in a rush I came away from Smith's with red ballpoints and so there are entire chapters in rubric. Hearing the recently dead speak is strangely moving. Muriel Spark, maybe, has a slight cold. Her eyes are weary and watery, and now and then she presses a tiny scrunched hanky to her nose. She is in Tuscany and her study window frames vignettes of the hilly landscape like those seen in the old masters' portraits of the Virgin. At one point she describes bombed London, the wallpapered rooms hanging in the air, the plants taking over, the intimate interiors open to every gaze.

Paul the Woodman, Paul the Organist

23rd May

No sooner had Paul the woodman reached his verdict and returned home with his 'Yes, I can manage that', though with no hard date, for although he was scribbling in his little book, he would not have entered Time or anything so committing, than the great willow spread its boughs wide and one fell down. It was perhaps a century old, rotten to the core though green-waving still. It seemed to be saying,

'Not yet, not yet!' But Paul was saying, 'Now'. Which might mean next month or next year. So he will eventually arrive to slice it up. When Richard Mabey was here I loaded his car with some weathered slices of another willow which Paul had felled ages ago. O willow, willow.

Stephen the organist from Brentwood came for our traditional walk to Wissington. It promised rain but held off. The Stour was a rich dark grey prinked, as Thomas Hardy would have said, with rising roach. Or maybe a wicked old pike. The maytrees were caked with erotic-smelling blossom and the mayflies danced dizzily around our heads. Mayflies are in three orders, nymphs, duns and spinners. Spinners do not eat. They spin around for a day or two then die. Flyfishers have little boxes of imitation mayflies, nymphs, duns and spinners, sometimes wearing them in their hats. We hung over the old Bailey-bridge and our faces warped and flowed in the current. We could have happily stood there for ever. Ambition, hunger, the afternoon, all drifted downstream. My having given poor Henry our vicar a list of hymns for our 'Songs of Praise' for him to put on the computer, Stephen and I talked vaguely about hymn language. But the mayflies and the deep river, between them, made us less than bright. I remember standing on Land's End when I was a boy and telling myself, 'Why do anything, why go anywhere? Why get a job?' The Atlantic crashed below, the thrift lay against my face, the gulls wailed.

At Wissington church we paid our spiritual dues to St Francis, smudgily preaching to the birds on the north wall, then sat on Paul Taylor's bench in the churchyard. It was where we always rested. 'Paul Rowland Taylor', it read, 'Royal

Air Force . . . killed in the Western Desert, aged 24. Organist. Oxford Scholar. Descendant of Dr Rowland Taylor, Martyr. May light perpetual shine upon him.' Our feet were careful not to tread down the bulldaisies and the speedwell. Wissington churchyard is exactly what a country churchyard should look like in late spring, patchy with flowers, sweet with thought. The south door to the church is almost exactly 1,000 years old. I imagined Paul Taylor sitting up there at the west end playing – what would he have been playing for Matins in late May? Christopher Wordsworth's 'See the Conqueror mounts in triumph'? Poor Paul, his life was as comparatively brief as that of the mayfly spinner.

Stephen and I progress through mud and nettles, and shimmering groves of youthful bat-willow, on the way home. The corn was being sprayed by Little Horkesley Wood. Still no rain. But clouds like dark changing promises were in high motion. Soon we are in Garnon's Chase, where John Constable walked to see his uncle and aunt, and where the ditches run fast with yesterday's downpour. Stephen is one of those peerless fellow walkers who is master of the companionable silences. Clad in shorts, he doesn't even cry out when the nettles embrace him.

The Hornets' Nest

28th May

Bank Holiday rains could not drown our fixtures. Bells crashed through them, cricketers played through them, visitors to the Flower Festival splashed through them, and the diocese will be solvent. Lakes appeared in the lanes. Ditches churned, boughs tumbled from trees in sheer wateriness. The flag on the tower wrung itself out time and time again. Tom brought his cows in. They who had only the other day run from their sheds in unutterable happiness now trotted to take thankful shelter from the wet outside world. But the sugar-beet swelled. My farm track rippled like a river and the ancient horse-ponds shone like slate.

Whether the bees and hornets in the larder were taking shelter it was hard to say, but a furious murmur met me when I entered it in search of marmalade. It is a long brick-floored room in which the tall fridge-freezer is in constant battle with the iciness of the larder itself. It was as I thought, a poor fat bee was glassily imprisoned on the washed jam-jars shelf, and I set it free by means of the classic postcard and tumbler method. When I returned the buzzing was still there, only now there was a great choir of it coming from all directions, a kind of orchestrated sibilance in which rage was being expressed symphonically. Thus, six times did I set both bees and hornets free, carrying them one by one into the garden, displaying immense courage. Meanwhile Henry our vicar was innocently laying a hand on an unseen hornet in the church, with dreadful result. Mercifully all he suffered was agony. Hornets provide a kind of first strike in the Pentateuch when God sends them before the Israeli forces to scare the enemy. They dwell peacefully in my vine, sunning themselves in the garden-lamp. No one knows a time when they were not there. But how could they not fly from a lidless jam-jar? Why did they come so near to death in their glass gaol when the door was wide open?

During rain pauses I begin the May weeding, sloshing about. The washed world smelled delicious. I leave red campion and cow-parsley among the garden flowers in order to attain my 'Giverny' effect. That shimmer of legitimate and outsider bloom which ravishes the late spring gaze. The freshly seen earth is rich and dark and, like me, soaked to the skin. For on days like these one does not become dry just because the rain has stopped. Richard Mabey has sent me some of his morning glories through the post, and I plant them in scrubbed orange pots, stick them with bamboo, and line them up with my sweet-peas. The white cat, who never minds a shower or two, paddles around.

All this done, having read a fine essay by Colm Tóibín entitled 'In search of the Writers of Aran', I find J. M. Synge's plays in the bookcase, where they have lain unopened by me. With the rain returned, I read the amazing *Riders to the Sea* and *The Playboy of the Western World*, forgetting time. Synge said, 'In a good play every speech should be as fully flavoured as a nut or an apple' – though many of his are as bitter as almonds. He was writing in Aran a hundred years ago, yet as modernly as any writer at this moment. The early deaths of his Aran men chime sadly with those in Iraq, 'whose families have been informed'. Well, that is something. The politicians who caused this disaster fly about the world.

Memory Maps and Marina Warner

2nd June

Memory is being re-examined. Loss of it is hugely dreaded in an age of aged people. Earlier in the year Marina Warner invited me to take part in her fascinating project of creating a database on the internet of what she calls Memory Maps, and I remembered what might be called a child's biography of the famous person in his home town. My celebrity was Thomas Gainsborough whose delightful statue in Sudbury stared over the market stalls to his birthplace, and about whom even as a small boy I began to collect all kinds of local information which art historians could never know. Most writers' memories are jackdaws' nests of infant as well as grown-up facts which are unlikely to separate themselves when they are grown up. One of my very earliest memories, perhaps when I was less than three years old, was of a disturbance in the night when a bird fell through the ancient chimney and beat, terrified, all around the room in which I was sleeping. Although there was no connection between this event and my mother telling me that my first word was 'dark', I did bring these two memories together in a short story. I had myself remembered the trapped bird but it was my mother, when I was adult, who had remembered as she and my father had gone to bed, carrying the oil lamp through the black house, repeating, as people do, the obvious. 'How dark it is,' one of them murmured. 'Yes, dark,' said the other. Then from the cot this first word, 'dark'.

Conrad adds a caution. 'In plucking the fruit of memory',

he warns, 'one runs the risk of spoiling its bloom.' Although the critic John Berger wrote that 'the camera relieves us of the burden of memory' – which I doubt – few of us, I fancy, are actually weighed down by what we remember. Selective, we are, certainly. Dismissive we are, humanly, of some of the memories, allowing them as little space in the forefront of our recollection as is possible. But the caring for and hoarding of small and precious memories is really a duty in each one of us, for it is these which re-shape art and philosophy, as Proust so dazzlingly taught us. Thus, as well as my frightened bird in the dark bedroom, when I was still less than three, I remember the smell of rotting plums in the dank grass and the nice stink of our pigsty, and the hard couch in Mrs Pleasance's cottage along the road, and the clank of pails at the pump, and being scared by geese.

The Bible has a vast amount to say about remembering but little about memory as we wish it to be. It requires us to remember God and later, and poignantly, to 'Remember me'. A small nation is told over and over again to remember its origin and its law, and individual men and women to remember their Maker. But Job confessed that 'when I remember, I am afraid'. And so too are we. Job comforted himself that 'my life is wind', and so too do we. But all through the Gospels those who had known the great Teacher, 'remembered what he had said'. Writers are always remembering what somebody said, what they looked like, what the time was, where they were, what they were thinking when they were buying cheese in Waitrose, which wasn't about the cheese. That now little-read novelist Dorothy Richardson described unstoppable memories and current thought as a stream of consciousness.

The Poet and the Woodman

4th June

What a day it was, yesterday that is. A shore wind took the burning edge off the June sun, the poplars hissed, the gliders floated angelically overhead, and I sowed two rows of Scarlet Emperor beans, one row of spinach-beet and lots of cucumbers. I also sent the organists the Trinity hymns and wrote an introduction to John Clare's holy sonnets. And cooked a chicken. I thought of poor young Richard Heber in the fierce Bombay heat and his early in the morning song.

Clare's holy song was not the official one. He sang out of doors and rarely in church. Sundays found him as far away as he could get from his parish in order to find what he called 'the eternity of Nature'. He was the outside worshipper whose creed was, 'Nature, thou truth from Heaven'. His fellow worshippers in this outside aisle were the kind of people who never got a Sunday off, shepherds and herdboys. Thinking of that distant scene my great-grandfather Charles, a Suffolk shepherd born in 1830, comes to mind. Shepherds did at least work but John Clare, skiving off every Sunday goodness knew where, did not do a stroke, hiding away in the ling with his hard hat as a desk. Once he wrote a tender hymn about 'An outcast thrown in sorrow's way'. This tragic Christ contrasts with his magnificent God the Creator. As for the Comforter, there would be long years in the poet's existence when he was absent.

Paul the woodman returned to see what he could do about the tumbling willow, a vast tree whose six branches were opening out like an enormous daisy, two of them towards the ancient bread oven. He stood there, pondering, then said that he would come back. No sooner had he disappeared than more branches fell, cracking a tile or two and swishing helplessly against the studio window like the biggest wiper in the world. Paul was interested in this self-destruction but reckoned that one of the still standing branches would be less beneficent and spoke of real damage. And so in five hours, his chainsaw moaning, the willow was slain. I gave him the ton or so of its wood and by teatime all that remained of a century-old tree was its hollow heart and sawdust. We mourned it in mugs of tea. 'How many cricket bats did I reckon they would get out of one of them bat willows down by the river? Guess.' Me – 'Twenty . . . ?' Paul, satisfyingly, 'Sixty to a hundred!' There were hundreds of bat-willows growing in the marshy grass by the Stour. They were a crop felled every fifteen or so years, and beautiful beyond words, the hazy joy of the Impressionists. But all those cricket bats in the growing, all those springing boundaries in the making! The plantations have been there as long as I can remember. From minute saplings just pushed into the earth – only they must touch the water line – to Lord's in the time it takes a player to grow up. Well, as Paul said, 'It makes you think.' Woodmen make you think, being philosophical by trade.

We all go to Esmé's ninetieth birthday party. She says, 'Don't think about the weather, I am having a marquee', and I imagine one of those elephant tents groaning from its ropes. But it is a canvas pavilion from the Field of the Cloth of Gold, open-sided and crowded. Half the congregation and half the part of Esmè's life we knew nothing about. What would John Clare have made of this sabbath happiness and its scent of crushed lawn, herbacious flowers and wine? He lived a long time in his madhouse, writing, writing sane words to 'my creator God'.

Worshipping the Unity

11th June

The heatwave has passed, was doused out of existence by brief heavy rains. It was a treat while it lasted – over a week – and I pretended to write in the garden even when the sentences were burned off the page as I scribbled them down. All the birds stopped singing and there was a blazing silence between dawn and dusk. The roses came out in force but the butterbur fell down in exhaustion. The horses swished each other under the may hedge. John mowed hay on the steep meadow, up and down, up and down, efficiently and that was all. No celebration. All rural celebration vanished when there was only one worker in a field.

A lovely hot Trinity Sunday with the church doors gaping and the extra candles wavering, and the remains of the Flower Festival giving off heavy scents. We sang 'Holy, Holy, Holy' and, as always, I thought of India. We 'acknowledge the glory of the eternal Trinity, and in the power of the Divine Majesty to worship the Unity'. The notices: the tower is to be re-pointed and so there may be interruptions to the bellringing. The tower is ancient beyond hard facts, its corners made by the Romans. They are Pompeiian red and flourish in the sun. We are in the presence of our Redeemer, Comforter and King, I tell the old friends in the pews, all twenty of them. I talk of Nicodemus, that cautious then wildly incautious follower of Jesus. Back home I de-nettle the honeysuckles and listen to Fauré, make cold soup and loll about. 'Trinity Sunday', I think.

A cluster of friends are leaving this world at the same time, although they are not aware of it. My prayers for them are rather like the school register. The more I consider such things, it is the last illness, not death, which is terrible for them. In each case it is cancer, with its conventional and non-conventional non-cures. I find myself contemplating death via that of these friends in a Franciscan manner, and accepting its naturalness, and attempting to see it through today's great cloud of 'treatment'. I feel little sorrow when the old die, more a sense of inconvenience when they can't come to supper as usual. But I am filled with sorrow for their last sickness and suffering, and pray for it to be soon over.

Some film-makers have come to make a DVD about the poet John Clare. They move the furniture around, put the outraged cat on the doorstep, light the scene where I am to sit on a great old wooden chair on which I rarely sit, and we begin. 'Say all you want to, we can always cut.' I have spoken so much about this writer that I am worried about sounding glib. His poetry and prose steadies my answers to the inter-viewer. His hawks and Northamptonshire birds of all kinds float in the air once more. The heatwave rain falls luxuriantly on the dense flowers beyond the window. The cross cat is let in. The cameraman talks of his two-year-old – Lewis, 'like in

Lewis Carroll', he explains. It is his birthday. He is two. He (father) must get back. The cat is five. I am – well, enough of that. The camera hums and the film lighting has done wonders for the ancient interior, causing it to look even older but sumptuously so. Later, I walk to the village shop with the laundry and the letters, splashing along.

The Death of Miss Helen Booth

13th June

I am walking to Helen's funeral. The afternoon air is moist and still. Birds sing loudly. Where the lane twists the hedge grows invisible under a mat of wild rose and traveller's joy. Fine stands of agrimony and mallow rear on its banks. Cars whisper by. Helen's cars, beginning with a Bullnose Morris and continuing with Estates, make ghostly journeys. She ceased counting after the very public centenary and withdrew to her slip of a bedroom, and was comfortable enough. Her mind revisited where she had been, who she had been. We visited her, myself careful not to harp on her age, for the worst thing about being over a hundred is being told how wonderful it is. It is not wonderful at all – just the persisting heart-beat and life not knowing when to stop. Just another day announcing itself through the thin curtain and jumping into one's consciousness like a jack-in-the-box.

We were old, old friends and Helen and her sister hardly more than middle-aged when I took my manuscripts to the post office. They would place them on the scales, give a start,

and tell me apologetically, 'I'm afraid it will be *Three and Six.*'
Behind them rose shelves sparsely arrayed with balls of string,
celluloid windmills, silvery baking tins, greaseproof paper and
towering pot-plants. They were the last of the Great War
entrepreneurial women whose smallholding skills – and fail-
ures – were plotted across the English countryside. In 1926,
when they were in their twenties, their father had sensibly
put them out to grass, so to speak, giving them seven acres
and a couple of clapboard cottages, sure that they would
make a go of it. And they did. Although never in any sense
mean, they were mistresses of the stretched funds of the inter-
war years. There was no tragedy in their lives. They were not
war-widows or war-bereaved fiancées but they did join the
army of men-less women which, with few qualifications, had
to make ends meet. Chicken-farms spread. It was a land of
wire-netting and chirping huts. Ladies in breeches lived on
shillings. They were the originators of today's farm-gate sales,
with their trays of vegetables and eggs at the roadside.

Helen and her sister, Win, began with chickens and ended
with cocker spaniels. In between there were ducks, geese and
goats. But it was by their kennels that most of the world of
country businesswomen knew them. They would show me
their Box Brownie snaps. There they were, being tugged along
traffic-less lanes by six dogs on a lead, their handsome faces
turned upwards, coins in their bags, and maybe their lips
learning lines for the current Dramatic Society play. For in
those days one had to be artful to a degree to escape having
a part in *Dear Octopus* or *The Mousetrap*. The world is divided
between these who seek a part and those who pray to God
every night not to be given one. Moreover, Wormingford in

those immediate post-World War Two days contained two dazzling and more or less inescapable village hall theatre directors, Christine Nash, wife of the artist, and Guy Hickson, brother of 'Miss Marple'. He too had a market garden by the side of the road. And now Helen, dear friend and relic of vanished activities, lay in her bright coffin as we sang, 'We love the place, O God' and the young gravedigger and his dog waited in the wings, so to speak. And Win, long dead, waited for her sister in the clay. And of course somewhere else.

Southwark

14th June

Could John Betjeman see me at this moment he would write a poem entitled 'Chapel Corner: the Last Passenger'. For I am waiting at the bus-stop where once I was part of a crowd of village travellers. Witty Jean, little Peggy from Newcastle, Mr West the Ayrshire dairyman, the grammar-school boy who is now a reverend, the assorted shop assistants and the aged man in his demob suit. And many others, all clutching their fares. Some have gone to paradise, some into smart cars. One or two have taken to bikes. Now there is only me. The stop has been called Chapel Corner for about a hundred years. Before this it was Bullocks Cross – presumably after the family which occupies Bullocks' Corner in Little Horkesley churchyard, the damp end where the snowdrops are at their best. The bus itself is part of my autobiography. Ages ago a young Cambridgeshire saddler journeyed our way and gave us this scarlet transport. I went to see my aunt on it when I was twelve, arriving with wet feet in the winter, having to tramp through river grass. She was an exact cook. 'Have you had your third parsnip?' In summer she plunged into the river wearing her one-piece costume to my great embarrassment. There was a conductor on the bus who shouted out, 'City centre!' when he came to his own village. In summer the laneside growth frothed against its windows.

But back to the now. I am off to Southwark Cathedral to do a kind of magic lantern lecture in the library. It is considered amazing by some of the neighbours that by standing at this stop I shall get there. In London it is hot and still. I wander like Keats towards St Thomas's Hospital, to 'where men sit and hear each other groan', then to the George, where stout businessmen in good suits, beautiful ladies with dyed hair, batches of Americans and Australians and lifelong friends sit at trestles in the yard. About twenty people smoke and the tobacco wreaths up to the moth-like planes which pass overhead every thirty seconds. I remember Little Dorrit, the bankruptcy heroine. Although we are all outside in the June evening, the air is stale and somehow 'experienced'. The old inn's galleries sag from the stagecoach luggage still, and maybe from the weight of English literature. At six-twenty I walk briskly to the Cathedral, nod to Shakespeare and meet the young Precentor. In his hand is Lancelot Andrewes's Bible. I can see the great bishop riffling its pages, finding texts for his Paul's Cross sermon. Early Trinity, so he may have been finding his way to Luke fourteen. 'A certain man made a great supper, and bade many ... Come for all things are ready. And they all with one consent began to make excuse.'

Andrewes taught George Herbert for a while – with this very
volume in his hand? Herbert went to the great supper, as we
know, astounded at having been invited. Eventually he
became to his delight the inescapable guest.

> All after pleasures as I rid one day.
> My horse and I, both tir'd, bodie and minde,
> With full crie of affections, quite astray;
> I took up in the next inne I could finde.
> There when I came, whom found I but my deare,
> My dearest Lorde . . .

Back home through the black garden to the white cat,
impeded by roses.

Jesu, the Very Thought of Thee

16th June

D evotion is not a word one would use religiously without
some care these days. Instead we talk of the, to me,
unpleasant occupation of churchgoing. Worship is also much
used. But when the old door closes and the bell stops we will
not be said to be at our devotions. Yet now and then something happens which sweeps past mere attendance and worship and takes us into the unguarded area of a one-to-one
love of Christ. Here we are, the worshipping collective, all on
our own with Him. A service barrier has fallen. And all this
because I had begun Matins with 'Jesu, the very thought of
thee' to Redhead, in which no tongue nor pen can describe
what we at this moment understand. That the love of Jesus,

what it is, none but his loved ones know. And this individually, not collectively. Old ghost stories often tell of meddling antiquarians releasing malign forces into the present. What Edward Caswall did when he translated the twelfth-century *Jesu, dulcis memoria* was to release something from long ago, something in abeyance yet untouched by time but simply waiting to re-invade the individual experience. He had joined J. H. Newman at Edgbaston Oratory where 'devotion' was the rule.

Some of us politely puzzle our non-churchgoing friends when we attend services. 'I mean', they say, 'he is just like us in most ways.' Meaning 'not obviously holy'. And indeed we frequently puzzle ourselves, intelligent beings that we are, when parish meetings and endless other activities become the inescapable concomitant of our religious life – indeed can almost submerge it. These spread from the pleasantly practical to the downright miserable. But then the washing-up and the book-keeping had to be done at Edgbaston, as at Bethany. Yet spare a thought for the beauty and passion of holiness. Give them time. Caswall's hymn pierces through all this and our worship this wet Sunday could have silently concluded after the last verse, our having this only joy, this prize, and this not congregationally but one-to-One. But of course we talk and pray and sing on. Yet the Jesu hymn won't leave our heads.

Shelley spurned the Christianity of his day. He wrote of:

> The desire of the moth for the star,
> Of the night for the morrow,
> The devotion to something afar
> From the sphere of our sorrow.

The old song which Caswall found is a love-letter to Jesus. Its purity and its tune makes us shed all our churchgoing inhibitions. I preach on George Herbert and his all-the-week friendship with Him. So more and more entirely personal letters. There they are, hand in hand, walking through the Salisbury water-meadows, exchanging love and advice, God and man enjoying companionship. There they are, singing Tallis in the Quire. There they are, at table, tirelessly talking, passing the bread. Halfway through my sermon I realise that it has become a literary lecture but there is no going back. And anyway, who can take in a word of it with no 'sweeter sound than thy blest name' still filling their heads? Our devotions over, we drive home. Small lakes lie in the lanes and our wheels make fountains. They brush escaped garden flowers and often have to be braked when we pass walkers. They know us – the churchgoers.

Lunch is Served

20th June

First the rain. It fell out of the sky in lasting douches, and was accompanied by sheet lightning which gave stagey glimpses of the surrounding hills. The farm track became as always a nice little river, the roses, Albertine, Cardinal Richelieu, Duchesse de Montebello, William Lobb, John Clare, etc. sopping wet balls. Old friends splashed their way across Suffolk for lunch, a semi-amphibious journey nobly undertaken. All went swimmingly until I turned on the electric oven to bake the fish-pie. I had been up since dawn making this. The guests were in the sitting room, Roy the wonderful Reader who has taught most of East Anglia what it is seeing when it comes to church, and our old friend Peggy who in a different sense has kept us in touch with our roots. Merry laughter in the next room. Then Gordon the churchwarden arrives, having found my glasses in his car. These are the pair I cannot actually see through and which I take around for fear of losing my best spectacles. All is perfectly timed. Wine is served. Fragments of useful information thread through into the kitchen. The table is laid. The salad is 'fatigued'. What an improvement on Barbara Pym, I think, whose hosts offer even the higher clergy sardines on toast and Nescafé.

Then the disaster. The fine newish stove has lost a timing button, without which nothing happens. I see just an empty socket. I crawl on the floor, move the cat, see the huge fish-pie cold and white. From next door I hear the enjoyment rising and I know that it has to climax in this extravagant dish. It is a quarter to one. And I cannot even heat the plates. I think wildly. Bread and cheese? As Christians, I tell myself, they have no option but to accept such a meal with grace – although it may not stop them from dining out on it when they get back home. Since there is no way of finding the tiny button, I turn my attention to the top of the stove, which works. Soon there are mushroom omelettes, new potatoes, peas, and plates hotted over boiling water. Meanwhile, after the party, the vast fish-pie asks, 'What about me?' Well, half of you can go into the deep freeze and the other half can last me until Sunday. I then search for the lost button, going so far as to empty the Dyson tube and pulling out the stove from its alcove. But no luck. There is St Jude of course but he has to deal with lost love, lost rings, lost hopes, and I don't like to bother him. The next morning, early, boiling days stretching before me, glancing down at the scrubbed brick floor, bright as a button, there it lies, the all-important missing agent. Well, thank God!

It is Flower Festival at Mount Bures, the loveliest in all England – which is not to decry other such events. But at Mount Bures, any Thomas Hardy character can stroll in and be immediately at home. Also it honours its patron saint, St John the Baptist. Was the Lord recalling what they said of Elijah – 'Then stood up Elias the prophet as fire, and his word burned like a lamp' – when he gave that dazzlingly brief obituary of his cousin, 'He was a burning and a shining light'? I expect so. My annual role in the Flower Festival is to take a sprig of St John's wort from my garden and put it by his statue above the altar. This is the species *Hypericum perforatum* with its radiant light holes which are not perforations at all but little resinous glands. But how it burns like a lamp to our seeking feet.

The Baptist and the Weeds

24th June

The Nativity of the Baptist – 'a burning and a shining light' – and our gardens at their zenith. Everything ten feet tall and perfumed. I walk through the early morning grass with bare feet, the cat in tow, the birds carolling, the day not yet made up its mind what to do, the kettle boiling, and last night's reading fluttering through a window. I am a little muddled, having returned from Stoke Charity in Hampshire, a June world of flashing trout streams, watercress beds and reed thatch whose lushness continues to demoralise me. I think of its treasure-box of a church in which all the coloured fragments of the old faith have been set out with a telling advantage. Ancient scraps of belief, bright and eloquent still. And a mile or so off the Roman road to Winchester, straight as a die and empty of traffic, the motorway robbing it of its function. At Winchester I stood in Bishop Ken's pulpit and thought of him teaching the boys his morning and evening hymns, and heard their long-vanished voices, each singing, 'Keep me, O keep me . . .' as they thought of the morrow's fishing.

Friends living in new houses built on old fields fret about weeds. They seem to think that they are blown in over the fence just to annoy them. But they are first-comers on their quarter-acres, plants which have been there since the year dot and which rose with the corn and never ended with its harvest. Sprays kept them under but – mercifully – did not destroy them. One has only to look at a set-aside field in June to see the vigour of its wild flowers, modest, un-admired things which hold on to their territory come plough or new housing. Traveller's joy round the edges, restharrow and ragwort at the centre, each saying, 'Escape me never!' I advise all those who garden what were for hundreds of years cornfields to read the poet Ruth Pitter's 'The Weed', and give up their dreams of horticultural perfection. Composed in what might be described as early Estuary English, this poem is defeatist stuff. Those who call every non-cultivated plant a weed are botanical racists. And here, in withering heaps, lie the horsetail and nettles I yanked up last night. I give them a wide berth with my bare feet in case they still have a sting in them. And here is a vast bush of St John's wort, the floral version of 'a burning and shining light', and laced through with raspberries. The trouble with plants is that they don't know their place. How dare a dandelion blaze among the sweetpeas!

Dame Julian saw Christ as a gardener. Did the Magdalen's brief mistake put the idea into her head? Julian saw God as the Lord of an estate and his Son as the gardener, 'digging and banking, toiling and sweating, turning and trenching the ground, watering the plants the while. And by keeping at this work he would make sweet streams to flow, fine abundant fruits to grow . . . I saw God's gardener as Adam, or in other words, Everyman'. She saw him dressed simply 'like a man ready for work . . .' Christ's sufferings began and ended – in gardens. His Father had put him to work in the garden of mankind, thought Julian.

Little Horkesley church clock says 'Seven' so it is time to stop counting the roses and to find breakfast. It is almost the summer solstice. There will be cards from the Mediterranean in the post. Bindweed grows through the wall and into the house. What a cheek. But I let it be. It does this every summer.

Lavenham Patron

25th June

Weather-wise, a chilly sandwich of wet winter between the airy warmth of late June. The old roses go wild, soaking up the rain. The horses in the briefly dank meadow lick the drops off each other. The cat, shocked, comes in. The next day, the sun out for all it is worth, I am taken to Lavenham as Patron of its Friends by the organist, who has a box of chicks on the back seat. They cheep helplessly. They are the kind which will lay brown eggs. We leave them by a coop of Buff Orpingtons and two or three football flags. Then to the stupendous church, the wool profits legacy of Tom Spring, Simon Branch and the thirteenth Earl of Oxford, who had sensibly gone into trade, though sprinkling his arms all over it to remind people that he was still far above Tom and Simon. On the way we drove past the Big Tree where as boys we met mother off the bus with the week's shopping. Being an elm, the Big Tree departed this life in the Seventies and just a few shoots which will come to nothing waver from its base. Lots of folk in church, lots of, 'Why, you haven't changed since last time!' and similar encouraging greetings. Outside in the churchyard lie generations of Romanies, including, I was told, lots of Petulengros. The turf is bubbling with topiary, and Peter and Paul have taken up residence once more in their niches over the porch. This vast Catholic building was finished just in time for the Reformation, just ready for Eamon Duffy's 'stripping'. Now there is a putting back. We sing:

Many a blow and biting sculpture
Fashioned well those stones elect,
In their places now compacted
By the heavenly architect . . .

and a sweet bell rings for the Elevation. I preach on Gratitude
as this virtue was exemplified by two women, Belgian Juliana,
the inventor of Corpus Christi (much to her convent's rage),
and an Aboriginal lady who was able to forgive what white
Australia did to her because she was given a New Testament.
This she combined with her ecological spirituality to make
a life well worth living. Now and then I remembered my
brother and I climbing the heady tower to emerge on the
leads, dusty white and triumphant to stare in all directions.
And once the verger hollering, 'Come you down!' Now, I am
at the altar with Father Nicholas where I could never have
imagined I would be.

At lunch in the village hall the blacksmith's daughter tells
me old tales. An aunt drove a great nail into the wall to hang
up a picture and it came through the other side. 'Never you
mind,' said her neighbour, 'I'll be able to hang my picture on
t'other end.' Lavenham is extraordinary. History by-passed it
after the Civil War. Were it possible for its wool-traders to
move back in they would find Lady Street, Water Street,
Prentice Street etc. much as they left them, though loomless.
A house without a loom, how puzzling. It would have been
like a man in some kind of existence without his heart.
Fr Nicholas and I drive back to Bottengoms via Tiger Hill
as the world gets ready for the immense rites of football.
What astonishes me is how men can shout for two hours
without drawing breath. How marvellous it would be if tiny,

poverty-stricken Ecuador won the Cup, I fantasise. How grateful would we be?

Unconsidered Grass

27th June

'All flesh is grass', wrote Isaiah in that ravishing fortieth chapter. He is singing about our impermanence and our permanence. Scripture is a very grassy way of looking at life as one would expect from its many pastoral authors. Micah's view of it as 'the showers upon the grass that tarrieth not for man' fits best these last few days. Briefly beaten down and flattened by the rain, it soaks the lower half of me before I have taken a dozen steps. Cold skies dull with unshed torrents stare across the meadows. Harriers fly low. Horses wear dripping blankets. But the short wheat remains upright like a dank but impervious green army. The hay harvest was over before all this. Its rattle-trap machine has been bedded down until next year. A blond evenness spreads where the grasses rippled. I scythe my hedge-bank and get wetter and wetter.

In church we have been reading Deuteronomy – 'My doctrine shall drop as the rain, my speech shall distil as the dew, as the small rain upon the tender herb, and as the showers upon the grass.' Outside it poured and poured, and umbrellas dripped in the porch. I spoke about the Baptist, the Lord's cousin, who was always out in the weather, good or bad. Water ran down the coloured glass but the bells spoke dryly and the graves sparkled.

The contract farmer has left a bit of the big field to do what it likes, so it has grown a grass crop which by dint of tallness has held itself up. It waves. It seeds. 'We are the True Fescues', it says. 'We are perennial. We shall come again.' Rye grass, darnel, meadow grass, sweet grass, quaking grass, here we sway. I remember the patch of quaking grass in the peggle-field near Chilton Hall when we were children, how it 'went' with bulldaisies. And lying in deep, deep grass in a kind of ceilingless grassy room and listening to the cows chomping nearby. Which is what the poet John Clare did when he wanted to write without being seen. I usually just read historical novels. The other day I found my *Anthony Adverse* book-marked with clover. The grass made a criss-cross pattern on my skin, got up my nose, got into my bliss.

Why did Walt Whitman call his poems *Leaves of Grass*? Did he see them as ephemeral or eternal? Their soaring American freedom enchanted me as a teenager. I have just re-read his wild Introduction to the first edition (1855). Is it possibly the world's best essay on candour? It takes one's breath away. We should look our rulers in the face and say, 'Who are you?' 'The prairie-grass dividing, its special odour breathing', Whitman drives us out into the open air, strips us of what we should not value, intoxicates us with weather, delivers us from 'the clank of the world'.

I gather some common quaking grass, the worse for wear due to the rain. I look it up in my Grass *Who's Who* in which the grassy language is a kind of faintly understood vocabulary which always makes me want several lives, this particular one for learning botany proper. Oh to speak '*Briza media*', with its beautiful 'long and wide, oval to heart-shaped, pendulous,

blunt, boat-shaped with shiny keels . . . flowering June–July'
in my track. All flesh is not this. I see grass dust on the Lord's
feet, grass pillowing his sleeping head. Here is some rye grass
which I haven't picked since I played Tinker–Tailor.

The Walking Christ

1st July

Two Evensongs, one at Westminster Abbey, where I preach
on 'The Walking Christ', one at White Colne, where I
talk about George Herbert. They are perfectly complemen-
tary. But how curious to be in London on Sunday afternoon.
I imagined that it would be empty, the City streets echoing
and walkable, but I had forgotten about the tourists, the pop
concert, the bombers and Ken's re-arrangements. Hundreds
of people in the Abbey and a choir like a great singing white
river, and all so beautiful, the praise, the movement, the
familiar faces in Poets' Corner, the mysterious man below the
poppies by the West Door, the English glory of the liturgy,
the dizzy pulpit, the Beatitudes set by Arvo Pärt. Unnumbered
comforts to our souls. And tall Canon Wright and a hurried
glance around the Jerusalem Chamber, and secret gardens
through windows, and the sixtieth Psalm – 'Who will lead
me into the strong city: who will bring me into Edom?' And
the gilded Plantagenets listening, Thomas Hardy too.

Faces from all over among the congregation. I spoke maybe
to weary sight-seeing feet. The Old Testament begins with a
man walking with God in a garden and in the New Testament

Christ's life ends with a walk along a rough old road. It was Sunday, and the divine companionship of Eden was renewed in the Jerusalem countryside. We are taught to think about the disgraced garden-dwellers but not about the loneliness of God when there was no one to walk with. 'O for a closer walk with God!' exclaimed poor William Cowper when mental illness seemed to drag him behind. More than once he fancied he was so far in the rear that he thought of killing himself. Illness causes us to lose step. Walking is notoriously curative. I once gave a talk to some Norfolk clergymen in which I recommended them to walk their parishes because (a) it was quite the best way to stay sane, and (b) it was the natural way to know and be known. I mentioned the Latin tag *solvitur ambulando* – you can work it out by walking – and they thought that they might give it a try. Cars and incumbents should not always go by in a blinding flash. Jesus said, 'I must walk today, and tomorrow, and the day after.'

And thus we drove to White Colne where I told the congregation about tall George Herbert on his horse. It was having tea in the churchyard and under racing skies. Nesting wrens above the south door squealed anxiously. King Wren. Most of the gravestones had long given up any information. The church was about the same size as Bemerton, only loftier. We sang, 'A man that looks on glass, on it may stay his eye' and the wrens concurred. I read Herbert's 'Even-song':

> Thus in thy Ebony-box
> Thou dost inclose us, till the day
> Put our amendment in our way,
> And give new wheels to our disorder'd clocks.

Poor young man, he was too ill to walk far, although he managed to tramp through the water-meadows to sing with the Salisbury choir every Thursday. His 'ebony box' was what awaited his disordered clock. He felt it ticking away, or rather working like a mole in his breast. At Westminster, where he went to school, I saw him running through the aisles and staring at the old glass, not all of it gone.

The Benson Medal

3rd July

A week in which the sun dominated everything, the funeral, the London visit, the landscape, my thinking. All except the ancient rooms which stayed cool and air-conditioned by history. Only now and then in the night did a beam complain. And now and then I watched a ball-game until the bawling crowds became intolerable. Today there was a kind of introit of impending change in the weather when a feeble croak of thunder and some sparkler-sized lightning occurred. A few penny-size raindrops hit the roses. But this was all.

The funeral was at the Crem and not in church, a long hot drive in the undertaker's car. It has a screen which reduces the mourners' cheerful talk to a sound like a distant aviary, and allows me to chat to the driver about his summer holiday. Kathleen awaits us at the Crem chapel. I did not know her, and assuming that few would at her great age I had written a kind of siblings' farewell, for she had still many brothers and a sister. I imagine a scattering of neighbours. She had been a businesswoman, a WAAF and, unbeknown to me, a woman who had 'kept up' with friends and colleagues from every stage of her life. Hence this truly sorrowful crowd, hence this strong singing, hence these tears. Outside the wreaths for her burned on the concrete. I read Donne's '. . . no noise nor silence, but one equal music . . . no ends nor beginnings, but one equal eternity'. The young men present were in dark suits with snowy open-necked shirts, the old men in what they believed to be smart casual, the women in flowery cotton. Kathleen – gone from her many offices.

Then to London to receive the Benson Medal for Literature. Beautiful travellers from all over are resting on the steps of public buildings, Hyde Park is gritty with red dust, the Serpentine is torpid, the flags limp, the heat Saharan, the Underground Dantean, but the National Portrait Gallery blissful as always. Faces – some of them as familiar to me as are those I have seen in the flesh. And praise God for Branwell Brontë's daubs of his sisters, and praise Him for old photos, and give moderate thanks for the official portraits of kings, and for the teashop and the quiet rooms. And praise Him for Shepherd's Bush, where I stayed overnight, sending myself to sleep with ancient copies of the *Scot's Magazine*. Who was the shepherd of Shepherd's Bush? Peter Ackroyd cannot tell me. Would he have been like the shepherd of John Clare's Langley Bush? Another poet, Edward Storey, wrote about the great transformation of this once rural peace from which Clare saw 'those uplands where the distant fields of corn often shone white with ripeness under a summer moon' and which is currently defaced by quarries and pylons. Not that I found Shepherd's Bush defaced but simply unknown. Unknown

squares, unsuspected silences, uninhibited splashes of garish-
ness and great distances through which the taxis cruise like
little clicking fish to gobble up the sun-weakened walker. The
enormity of London!

Back at Bottengoms Farm I throw myself, although this
isn't quite the right word, into summer clearance, mowing
the always dank grass, for no sun has ever got the better of
this rivery patch, tugging handsome stands of hogweed out
of the gunnera. This mighty-leaved plant is named after
Bishop J. E. Gunner from Sweden. It thrives where my stream
debouches into the horsepond. And thus, the heat prevailing
still, I brush the exhausted insects from my hair – including
a hornet.

Bury St Edmunds, Market Day

7th July

To the Friends of St Edmundsbury to preach on the Conversation of Jesus. Heavens, what a lot of them there
are, a whole cathedral-ful. The heatwave is in spate but the
cathedral is high and cool, and we process in to George
Bell's 'Christ is the King, O Friends rejoice!', the choirboys
surreptitiously fanning themselves with service-sheets and the
rest of us bearing up beneath our robes. It was Bishop Bell
who invented 'Friends' during the Twenties when he was
Dean of Canterbury, and now that they have spread from
churches to gardens, to zoos and every institution imaginable,
and even to Wormingford's St Andrew's, it is impossible to

imagine any edifice without them. Somewhere in that listening crowd are about fifty people I know but all the faces have become impressionistic dobs of Chinese white in the swirls of summer clothes, and I have to stop wondering if my elevated Pauline talk can be heard below the pulpit cushion. 'Meditate, and show the kind of young man you are by the way in which you *talk*,' said the aged Apostle to Timothy.

Lunch afterwards in the marquee, the carpets rambling over the builder's gravel, for we haven't quite finished the tower. Having had the heatwave for getting on for a fortnight, it is becoming normal to burn. But the town's character is quite altered. Being Saturday several thousand folk have decided to saunter around in as little as possible and there is great idleness. Being early for the cathedral, I add my own bone laziness to it by taking my place on a scorching seat beneath a nice tree where two large retired villagers are word perfect on the failings of farmers. Their conversation is a kind of Suffolk Beckett as it rumbles to and fro. And ending of course with, 'You never see a farmer *on a bike*, do you?' 'Well, you never see a farmworker on a bike', I could have interrupted, but who am I to put an economic spanner into this good grouse? Nearby a girl flies into the arms of a lad. Then an ancient chap wheels a text into our vision. It says that each one of us will have to acknowledge our sins before God. I do a bit of shopping, curtain-rings and cheese, just the essentials. The pedestrianised streets and squares are crammed with stalls. Nobody calls out as they once did. 'Polstead cherries, Polstead cherries, red as Maria Marten's blood!' Those were the days. Just up the road is the prison where poor Bill Corder swung for her. Those were the days.

At lunch I sit with kind Bishop Lewis and we speak of his native Cornwall. And I have a sudden desire to be there again. I can hear the Atlantic beating against the rocks and smell spindrift, and feel the perilous edge of the cliff – and the freezing cold of the granite aisle at the Eight o'Clock. One should now and then, though not make it a habit and be thought scatterbrain, take the next train to Penzance on the spur of the moment. But here I am at the Bishop's table and politely chattering to the Friend next to me about the sugar-beet factory, the highest thing in Bury St Edmunds before we built the cathedral tower. Did he remember how the beet would tumble from the laden carts? Did I remember how boys on bikes on the way to school would hang on to the sugar-beet carts and get a free ride? How could we forget it! How could any of us forget anything? A few yards away is the house where Defoe wrote. It occurred to me to make an aside during my 'Conversation' sermon to inform the choir boys that he called his poor castaway Robinson Crusoe after a boy in his class, but then I thought that this might be *too* conversational. *O sacrum convivium* we will soon be singing.

Jane and Orlando

15th July

The unimaginable day has arrived. Tony drives me to Addenbrookes Hospital to say our goodbyes to our oldest friend. Sun-whitened grasses along the track down which she would speed to the house shake as we pass. Scabious is picking itself up after a brief battering rain. The lanes are fresh and airy. I have this sense of gladness after the doctoring is done and I try to feel sad. Although the real sadness always comes to me later, when again unimaginably it is no longer possible to ring up. However, off we go to Cambridge, zipping along the dead straight Newmarket road in a very lively fashion quietly wondering what we will find at the end of the journey. On Sunday I had spoken those peerless words over the kneeling figures – 'O God, the protector of all that trust in thee, without whom nothing is strong, nothing is holy; increase and multiply upon us thy mercy; that, thou being our ruler and guide, we may so pass through things temporal, that we finally lose not the things eternal . . .' Hospital car-parks everywhere will be filling up with Get Well cards and farewells – and heat, for the summer is making a come-back.

I have been enthralled for days on end by a photo of Mozart's wife. There she is in the flesh, his adored Constanze, caught just as she was by the falling shutter and quietly looking out of the *Guardian*. She is seventy-eight, he was thirty-five. It is like seeing Anne Hathaway. Painted likenesses fall away from this snapshot, or rather carefully grouped family, for Constanze is staying with the Kellers at Altotting, Bavaria. Her parted hair is suspiciously black for such an old lady, her expression is quietly intelligent. I look and look at her, the lover of that wild young man, the mother of all his children, the listener to the *Requiem* as it tumbled daily from his bed. I possess an 1850s photo of a German wedding. It shows what looks like a teenage bride and groom about to get into the honeymoon carriage, and it is a novel in itself. One may read and read into it. The new husband wears a stovepipe hat, the new wife a crinoline. They look fragile, the horses look impatient, the street looks waiting and empty. What happened to them? Where were they? So thin and young, so trapped in clothes, so unsmiling, but with their shadows on the ground.

I have taken The Naming of a Child service for Orlando (and a string of delightful other names which are going to give him trouble when he has to fill up forms), and the country church becomes exotic with Londoners. Orlando's grandmother reads from the Prophet Kahlil Gibran, who rightly tells us:

> Your children are not your children.
> They are the sons and daughters of Life's longing for
>   itself . . .
> You may house their bodies but not their souls,
> For their souls dwell in the house of tomorrow, which you
>   cannot
> visit, not even in your dreams . . .

Orlando, who is one, gazes about him with jewelled eyes. We all sing. 'He gave us eyes to see them' (each little bird that sings) and a girl films us for when we are no more. I walk to the barbecue through the hayfield, my cassock trailing in the seeding plants. What else did the Prophet say? 'For life goes not backward nor tarries with yesterday.' I am a great tarrier with yesterday I have to confess.

Not to be Missed

18th July

It is a salutary thing to confront a measure of one's personal intolerance. Here am I on the London train getting steamed up because the couple opposite are watching a screen and not the passing view. Have they not heard of the stream of consciousness? 'The what?' I hear them reply. My heart softens towards them and hardens towards myself. And to put myself right I look out on what I must have looked out on all my life, the sixty or so miles between the Essex–Suffolk border and Liverpool Street. Here are the stops where I have never left the train, the trees I have never seen except through glass, the little gardens which are almost as familiar to me as my own. And of course, jungly in July, is the glorious railtrack growth which Richard Mabey calls the unofficial country-side, the flowers and fruit which will never be gathered, the forests of the sidings, and the ruthless take-over of the lovely buddleia, the butterfly-bush. What a long way this plant has come since the French missionary Père David found it on the Tibetan–Chinese border in 1869. The world's railways were new-fangled then and their hard lines in need of nature's softening hand.

I am soon lost in reverie on a London trip. Here is, under this water-meadow, the capital of Cymbeline. Here is Witham, where Dorothy Sayers, commuting to Benson's in the Strand, climbed into the carriage and spent her journey working out what next to do with Lord Peter Wimsey. Here, across the fields near Chelmsford, is the palace of New Hall from which

Prince Charles and George Villiers, calling themselves Smith, rode all the way to Madrid to bring back the Infanta. It was the far chimneys of this house which began to create in my head a novel called *The Assassin*. Here is the King Harold pub where Benjamin Britten would ritually stop to have a pint on his drive back to Aldeburgh. Here is Brentwood where Stephen plays the organ. Here is Romford, home of that excellent poet, Ruth Pitter. Here is Bryant and May's match factory where all the poor Victorian women got phossy jaw, and where they held a great strike.

Inevitably early in London, I go on little explorations in the City, Southwark, Westminster, anywhere within the sphere of my appointment. And thus, although not in the Peter Ackroyd league, I have become a tolerably good London historian although I have never lived there more than four consecutive days in my life. The train's stream of consciousness debouches into the life which flows through streets. Doctor Johnson's familiar mot that he who is tired of London is tired of life had received a strange poignancy by my glimpsing on television his death mask, or in fact his death torso, for the wax had spread from his poor face to his naked breast. Accustomed to his marble bareness, which is likeness enough, this immediate post-death-and-suffering impression of his flesh destroyed time and art. So this, I said to myself, is what Samuel Johnson looked like. Here was his infirmity and his strength. Having looked unwell all his years, he looked in death much as he had always looked, and as he would have looked rolling along the Strand. But soon, in next to no time at all, I was back home where days can pass without so much as a dog-walker passing, but where the dream persists, that constant action of the mind which speeds up on the station and positively races on the concourse, and which falls to brooding in alleys.

Captain Cardy Ploughing

20th July

What with weather, what with machinery, farmland soon becomes out of knowledge. I have two acres and all the other acres grow around me. The contours stay mainly unchanged yet at the same time mysterious. There is a slight amphitheatre-like rise above Lower Bottoms and what must have been a Slough of Despond in the Top Field for many a plough. The old Horseman (East Anglian for ploughman) tells me how it was when he drew his first furrow, setting it against a holly bush in the distant hedge. Hedgers never levelled a holly and I see them round the village still, many of them tall trees. 'It would have been about February', said the Horseman. And I see the Horseman as a slight youthful figure hip-hopping along behind his Punches, the plough tipping and reeling, its share striking sparks from the everlasting flints.

In the late nineteenth century, during that nadir of English agriculture, with even the horsemen, the princes of the fields, broken and half beaten, Henry Rider Haggard, who farmed in the Waveney Valley, watched the February ploughing with humility, familiar as he was with it. As with our present summer, it rained and rained although with less eventual ruination of rural life. He had spent his twenties in South Africa filling his head with the tales which would become *King Solomon's Mines* and *She* (who must be obeyed). Then it was back to Norfolk and this shocking sight of white men in the mud. His men, his demanding fields. It was 1898 when farmworkers, even the noble horsemen, were all lumped together in the popular mind as labourers, skill-less creatures whose duty it was to simply toil. While Haggard was shocked by their servitude, he began to see their art, for their work was nothing less. He wanted to destroy the huge social barriers which cut him off from his men but it was not only impossible but unthinkable. In an Egyptian pyramid he had seen a beautiful fresco of a king and his harvesters all rejoicing in a field together, the corn shining in their arms. If only Norfolk could be like this! If only his labourers would speak to him! He could afford to pay them twice their wage but it would put Norfolk's economy out, of course. So he told the world how they work, with what brilliance, with what strength.

'Ploughing is one of those things that look a great deal easier than they are, like the writing of romances. The observer, standing at a gate to watch a man with a pair of horses strolling up and down a hill for hours on end . . . is apt to conclude that beyond the physical endurance involved the difficulties are small. Let him take the pair of horses, however, and plough for, say, forty minutes, and he will come away with a greatly increased respect for the ploughman.'

As boys we watched Captain Cardy's plough surge to the headland like a tall clomping horse-wave, wheel and flood back. He had fought on the Western Front and I always imagined to myself the jingling of the horse-brasses with the jingling of his medals. He did not call out to us. The irony was that when all the young men fled the collapsing farms for the glory of soldiering they were set to digging trenches, vast ditches made with spades by regimented labourers. The Horsemen rode. Nobody dared beat their bayonets into ploughshares. Everyone dreamed of their own church bells and forgot their own ditches and bush-draining. From no-man's-land they dreamed of someone's-land. When I went to see Passchendaele some years ago, it was drizzling but the mud was unlike the mud here. It was silvery in the trodden grass.

Henslow's Outing

23rd July

Stephen and I are having one of our Suffolk meanderings when all at once a signpost waves to us. Hitcham, it says, come to where one of the mightiest of all village outings took place. The rain-filled skies are low and propped up by oaks and church towers, and the windscreen wipers click fretfully. But here, and all unplanned for, lies Hitcham. And here in my memory are dull Sundays in Cambridge marvellously enlightened the moment I open the gate of the Botanic Garden with the Sunday Key which has been loaned to me by my friend Denis Garrett the celebrated mycologist. Once created, the question arose whether it would be breaking the sabbath to visit it on a Sunday, and this key was given to people who could be trusted to do this without enjoyment.

But we are about to visit the parish of the wonderful John Stevens Henslow who practically single-handed removed a small physic garden in the middle of Cambridge to some forty acres of farmland along Trumpington Road and thus formed one of the world's finest botanic centres. He arrived at Hitcham in 1837 to discover a wretched village of warring farmers and child labour, and left it with a good school, allotments, cricket and athletic clubs and a history of railway excursions, the great one being that of Thursday 27th July 1854 when he took no fewer than 287 Hitchamites to Cambridge to see his Botanic Garden. He gave each one of them an eleven-page booklet which he had written and illustrated – he was a splendid botanical artist – and they all arrived at Cambridge Station at 9.20 a.m. They walked the Garden, had dinner at Downing College at 2 p.m. and in effect, due to their formidable and scholarly rector, had their lives changed.

As did an undergraduate named Charles Darwin. Henslow was only thirteen years Darwin's senior. Together they laid the foundations of the neglected science of botany and natural history as they explored the Fens, the college gardens and in the vacations further afield. When Henslow was asked to recommend a naturalist for a ship called the *Beagle*, he recommended Charles Darwin. Unknown to both of them, the voyage of the *Beagle* would shake Christianity to its foundations. On Henslow's memorial in Hitcham church, by way of the usual flourish, we are required to look up Job 29. Which Stephen and I did in what we thought must have been John Henslow's own lectern Bible. It is the passage in which Job recalls his own honourable conduct, 'I delivered the poor . . . and him that had none to help him . . . I caused the widow's heart to sing for joy . . . I was eyes to the blind, and feet was I to the lame . . .' And no country clergyman could have done more for all his parishioners than this brilliant botanist. It took him out of Cambridge of course, and there were moanings at this. He died aged sixty-five and lies in the churchyard there in Hitcham, and under the nearly bursting rain clouds, a hero of mine.

In his *Autobiography* (1873), Darwin wrote of his old friend, 'His judgment was excellent and his whole mind wellbalanced, but I do not suppose that anyone would say that he possessed much original genius.' But as a recent Director of the Cambridge Botanic Garden rightly observed, 'Without Henslows there are no Darwins.' Some time ago, recalling the Hitcham excursion, I took a dozen or so of our parishioners to walk in the lovely intellectual Garden, and must do so again.

The Outside Worshipper

25th July

Observing the white night at 3 p.m. I can see the heat resting, as it were. The corn is solid gold, huge still wedges of it fitted between the headlands, and the garden flowers remain open. There is no dawn chorus but here and there I can hear a listless soloist. Two horses talk to each other beneath a maytree. Should I get up and write? Should I lie back in the cool ancient room? Should I listen to horrors on the bedside radio? Should I make a sound, the cat will dash in for breakfast. My oldest friend has died, should I mourn her? At ninety-one? Come, come! I can hear her. 'Try not to be silly, dear.' I will read John Donne's soliloquy at her committal, the one about 'coming to that holy room, Where . . . I shall be made thy music'. But fancy dying during such a summer.

To Helpston for the 25th John Clare Festival. The handsome stone village burns in the sunshine, his cornfields too. The barn in whose threshing dust the poet wrote a little algebra with his finger is like an oven. His birthplace would be unrecognisable to him, so white and smart, his pub too with its lavish ploughman's lunch and crowd of authors. But here is his great (several greats) grandson, and here are his readers come to do him honour. Homage-paying literary societies must have begun in the Mermaid after Shakespeare had departed. Or possibly in Athens when Sappho had gone to Olympus.

I had to write about John Clare's faith. His Church was out of doors. He describes it constantly. Like William Wordsworth, he drew his beliefs from 'Nature and her overflowing soul'. Clare was the outside worshipper and poem after poem of his delights in the freedom of the sabbath fields and hearing distant bells. His creed began, 'Nature, thou truth from Heaven'. His fellow worshippers were shepherds, gypsies and herdboys, though mostly he preferred to sing alone amidst birds and flowers. The annual cycle of growth, the seasonal weather and the continuity of creatures and plants in more or less the same few acres witnessed to him the eternal. In fact he summed up his religion in a long statement entitled 'The Eternity of Nature', and in a perfect epigram for himself:

> He loved the brook's soft sound,
> The swallow swimming by;
> He loved the daisy covered ground,
> The cloud bedappled sky;
> To him the dismal storm appeared
> The very voice of God . . .
> A silent man in life's affairs,
> A thinker from a Boy,
> A Peasant in his daily cares –
> The Poet in his joy.

In a tender hymn, 'A Stranger once did bless the earth', he saw Christ as 'An outcast thrown in sorrow's way' and this tragic figure contrasts with his magnificent God, 'creator of Nature'. Even when cast into the very depths of this world's suffering, in Northampton Asylum, Clare was kept sane by the huge truth of 'my Creator God'. He and 'the insects in the brake' were brothers.

Summer Cleaning – and Vikram Seth

27th July

A home and away week. Without thought and minus planning I turn out the larder. It is one of those rambling rooms tacked on to the farmhouse proper in the eighteenth century. It is also temptingly accommodating so that eventually it will contain a great many un-larderish items whose mouldy breath brings a whiff of mortality to the true inhabitants of this space, jams, wines, strings of onions and a nice bit of cheese. Thus, with the combine harvester passing and re-passing the north window, I bravely lift the lids of ancient preserves, amass old tins which will never see the oven again and, eventually, scrub the dipping brick floor with spring water – the kind which people so strangely glug from bottles on trains. It is late July. The combine trundles into view every few minutes in a haze of wheat dust. It puts on airs, pretending to be a cornucopia, the grain shooting out with cries of Plenty. It leaves blond streaks across the landscape as it appears and disappears between my toppling willows. A delicious new scent, one I haven't sniffed for years, fills the larder, the smell of scrubbed boards and bricks. As for the hot summer's day, it has passed, as has the harvesting man for the last time. I take my decidedly unwashed self to the edge of the field to gaze forth in weariness, having carted all the junk which a larder should not shelter to a shed, where it can go on mouldering with impunity. A startled green woodpecker gives a loud ringing 'laugh' as it zooms from its cover and undulates into the open. 'What a fuss', says the white cat. This week's bed is an old stone sink lined with stonecrop.

Away to Salisbury. Only the green woodpecker's flight is faster. The Waterloo train is air conditioned and blissful. Basingstoke, Whitchurch, more mown fields, great heat the other side of the glass, then the start of the chalk cuts, then the glimpse of the cathedral spire. I walk to Sarum College, make sure that my notes and readings are the right ones, then stroll across the languid grass to the West Door. What Mrs Proudie would have said one would not like to imagine. The lazing populace, the supine blokes, the abandoned ladies, the tentative lovers, the toppled children, the dogs doing what they liked, the correct describer of this sun-felled scene would not of course have been Trollope but Traherne, the poet of Christian delight, the master of enjoyment, the commender of summer sloth. But also the insister of intellectual awareness. 'To think well is to serve God in the Interior Court.'

Wandering through the cathedral I think of John Constable painting it and George Herbert singing in it. I hear the stops and starts of choir practice. I gape at the amazing, unbelievable vaulting, I peer at Magna Carta, the thirteenth-century thickly written piece of A4 vellum in its glass case, then take a seat. I allow architecture to exclude the sun. A young tourist asks me about cadavers and I explain. As I am so shalt thou be. He and I – so clearly everlasting? The choir continues its broken psalm. 'Try again, "With long life will I *satisfy* him" – once more.'

After the reading in Sarum College Vikram Seth and Judy Rees carry me off to Bemerton. We cross Herbert's garden and walk rather perilously – it is getting dark – over the unrailed bridge which spans the Nadder. The air is heavy with meadow-sweet. We come to a second, safer bridge and pause, breathing in the night-time. I can hear nesting birds talking to each other. Vikram talks about the pike which lurk in the black water. He himself is full of light. Indoors he reads to us from Izaak Walton.

The End of Cathedral Camps?

7th August

Having made my last visit as Patron to the last of the Cathedral Camps, albeit in the Tractarian glory of St Mary's Bourne Street and St Barnabas's Pimlico, those red-brick parish churches whose exteriors give little hint of the splendours within, I tried to think of a suitably Tractarian conclusion to what we had achieved. 'We' being the articulators of Robert Aagaard's inspiration, which was to send groups of young people from all over the world on polishing, dusting, redecorating, scrubbing working holidays into every cathedral, there to clean things which not even the most dutiful verger could be expected to reach. We gave them hard hats, those moving towers for getting to the still heights, scarlet T-shirts, portable showers, conservators to show them how to wipe the grime of centuries from some ancient face and good leaders. Thus, August after August for twenty-five years I have gone to cathedral after cathedral to praise their unique toil. But now, it is said, the world has changed, the labourers are fewer, the insurance dizzier, the concept fulfilled.

My friend Alan Webster involved me in this exercise. He said how Robert Aagaard during the early 1980s had put together a formidable cathedral-cleaning group of fund-raisers, deans, clerks of works, architects, writers, artists, conservationists and experts on cleaning materials and safety harness to get his dream going. Young people from every faith and none were, every August, on their knees in Anglican quires or perched like angels in towers and clerestories. Until a few months ago I thought that it could go on for ages to come. But no. 'To every thing there is a season, and a time to every purpose under the heaven.' A time to beeswax the stalls, and a time to cease beeswaxing the stalls. 'All go unto one place, all are of dust, and all turn to dust again.'

But not, surely, these Spanish, English, American, French, Scottish boys and girls resting round the vestry table in St Mary's, Bourne Street? How could they ever fade? Tractarian cleaning, I should add, is quite unlike other cleaning. You need finicky fingers for Comper and Bodley. They have removed the dirt from the golden and red baroque of the soaring reredos and gently wiped the suffering figures with cottonwool. They have gone as far as they can reach, which is as good going as any of us can hope for. A camper apologises for not reaching the 'swan' on the font cover. Gently, I tell her the story of the pelican in its piety. In St Barnabas I think of John Keble, John Mason Neale, Pusey and Manning leaning from the stone pulpit. Tonight the campers will have a barbecue in the courtyard, with the Son of Consolation looking down and the Pimlico residents wondering what is going on. Where Anglo-Catholics are concerned there is apt to be always something going on. Our Stour valley churches know how to rise to the occasion – and how to sink back into their vast history. Only poets and saints can hear and see what happens in-between services.

London teems with summer. It smells of hot stone and burning leaves. 'Here is the library,' says Ed the camp leader, and I enter a Victorian room. 'We sit here', he assures me, 'and read.' Of course, what else? Is that Newman's *Apologia pro Vita Sua* glinting behind the bookcase glass? Below in Bourne Street the traffic drifts home. No more trips to Cathedral Camps, High Church or Low Church. And what will we do with all the left-over polish?

The First Love-letter from the USA

12th August

To neighbouring Boxted to praise its new history book and to tell what the population already knows. The sun, the architecture, the Matins, the congregation come together in a kind of English perfection. Denise the Reader carries us through the service with native simplicity. The choir sings from the west gallery, clear-glass makes rainbow colours on our faces. 'New every morning' indeed. It was not so when Mr Phillips abandoned Boxted Vicarage in April 1630 for Massachusetts, he and his wife and their children, and this now exquisite parish church was left a poor grubby muddle of cracked artefacts and religious notions. I have often imagined the Great Migration of the Godly Folk of the Stour Valley as they heaved their families, best beds and seedcorn on to the wagons and trundled away to found the United States of America. They sailed on the *Arabella*, their children and creatures dying all the way. Their leader, Mr Winthrop, arranged that his wife should follow on another ship. He wrote:

> Mine own, mine only, my best beloved. Methinks it is
> a very long time since I saw or heard of my beloved,

River Diary

> and I miss already the sweet comfort of thy most desired
> presence, but the rich goodness and mercy of my God
> makes supply of all wants. He sweetens all conditions
> to us, he takes our cares and fears from us. He will
> guide us in our pilgrimage. My dear Wife, be of good
> courage: it shall go well with thee. Once again let us
> kiss and embrace. Your ever John Winthrop.

I suppose that this could be the first love-letter from the States. The Boxted seedcorn was not dressed, of course, so up came all the Boxted wildflowers as well as the first harvest, scabious ('nops'), corncockle, fine thistles. In New England they gave the fled Vicar of Boxted thirty acres by the Charles River. They said that he was 'the earliest advocate of the Congregational order and discipline'. And here am I in his pulpit, under his forsaken roof, half-blinded by his sunshine.

I dash to London for a meeting at Southwark Cathedral, arriving ages before I am due. So I stroll through Tooley Street and beyond about breakfast time, catching sight of the Tower of London as it appears and vanishes between office cliffs. It looks like a pretty toy, as does Tower Bridge. The Thames clearly flows from Iceland. Still too early for business, I enter the Cathedral and read every wall plaque, spinning them out, translating merchants' Latin, nodding to Shakespeare's brother in the Quire, hearing the gasps of the Marian martyrs as they are sentenced behind the high altar, watching the huge floor-polishing machine making the aisles shine. Now it drones around Lancelot Andrewes, now round the beautiful woman who is gazing and still, the only worshipper at the moment. Committee members arrive. It is a great day. Cathedral Camps is to be saved from oblivion. Too wonderful to vanish after only twenty-five years, it will go ahead under CVS – and who or what better? As we used to say, 'It has gone to a good home.' Thus we celebrate.

Compostings

15th August

Three old friends have been grave-hunting, returning jubilant. They have purchased three neighbouring graves, at £400 apiece, in one of those woodlands which cover you up in a nature burial spot not far from the Suffolk coast. They talk headily of silver birches and broom, of whispering grasses and humming bees. Twice have I laid to rest bodies in such places, one of a young farmer, one of an ancient historian, his in Essex, hers in Cambridgeshire, and each time the funeral was extraordinarily beautiful and sacred. God being its Creator, can there exist an inch of unconsecrated ground? Defiled ground, certainly, but who is to blame for that? However, being a chronic churchyard walker and tomb-taster extraordinary, I can see that this nature burial business is going to deprive me of my recreation. Last Sunday, for instance, I discovered in a churchyard near here, 'Nathaniel aged 17 and his wife Ann . . .' Now there's a story. And yesterday we laid my neighbour Leonard between a babble of local headstones, all of them communicating the village, and strolling past his house his nice dog gave me its customary bark.

These serious matters completed, the white cat and I lie on the grass and read a French novel, the summer having returned. Oh, how blissful to be on top of the earth, to feel the sun hot on one's skin, to see the pages flutter in the warm wind, to hear the squirrels scurrying for nuts and to watch the cloud Himalayas through one's lashes. I had read John Donne's 'Bring us, O God, at our last awakening into the house and gate of heaven, to enter into that gate and dwell in that house, where there shall be no darkness nor dazzling, but one equal light' and now I smelled something so paradisal as to make me sit up and lose my place. My head had been touching the wild pea which David had brought from Tuscany years ago, and whose seed I religiously gather every autumn. Twenty or more purple flowers and their marvellous scent were suddenly 'out', and for all their worth. I imagined the Florentine artists, in search of pigments in August, having a rest against a rock and drawing up this same perfume, and feeling immortal.

The rain gone, the harvest arrives. Mr Bradshaw has taken his oil-seed rape, harrowed-in its hull and left a fine emptiness, acres and acres of light brown soil all neat and tidy-like, as they say. Soon the combines will be let out of their dark barns to gnaw wide paths through the wheat. A month of rain, and now the fields look as though they wouldn't mind a little drink. People are on holiday or toiling unsociable hours. Organists are at a premium. Sometimes we sing the hymns unaccompanied and say the liturgy alternately. I rather like these spare Matins and Evensongs. They are like interior retreats.

I must weed, not the garden but the bookcases. They bulge and sway, topple and protest. Not another volume. And I hate a tight shelf. So a hard-hearted sheep and goats business is called for. Or of course some more bookcases. And it takes such an age, this sorting, what with the reading and the absence of ruthlessness. Here is a fascinating edition of Helen Hanff's (*84 Charing Cross Road*) *Apple of my Eye* ... And now it is lunchtime for man and beast, the latter jumping up and down with greed.

Roger Dying

21st August

We sit by Roger's deathbed, Alison, Vicki and I. It is late Sunday afternoon with the heatwave fading, and Roger lies against a white mountain of pillows. The little window opens on to the mite of grass and the cool moat in which Roger swam all the year round, writing the Preface, as it were, for his strenuous masterpiece *Waterlog*. Now he whispers, his famliar voice a kind of human susurration in tune with aspen leaves, and we listen hard to catch his words. He looks if anything rather astonished, as do we in our different ways. When he drove from his ancient farmhouse to mine he would bring a present, a fine cup, a fine grapefruit sapling he had grown from a pip, and once a wonderful new scythe from Stowmarket. Now and then we were made to stand side by side at literature festivals and talk about the countryside and he would laugh because, he said, I used complete sentences, 'the kind you read'. And now his light flickers, every now and then flaring into his old self, every now and then on the verge of going out. The rough draft for the jacket of his last book slips on the coverlet. It is called *Wildwood: A Walk through Trees*.

I have brought John Clare's poems with me. I read the one which Ted Hughes read in Poets' Corner when we put up a memorial to him. It is called 'The Nightingale's Nest' and it describes Clare being torn between his need to come close to the sitting bird and his longing not to scare it. How can he communicate his not being like other men, or rather boys? It is a long poem and Roger's ears, I realise, are not at all dying at this moment. He is listening to Clare as keenly as we listened together to the nightingales at Tiger Hill. Both John Clare and John Keats – they knew of each other and shared the same publisher – believed that the nightingale 'lived on song'. Clare was the greater naturalist and knew all about those physical things which produced the music, the dense coverage below the trees in Royce Wood, the secret nest:

> . . . no other bird
> Uses such loose materials or weaves
> Their dwellings in such spots – dead oaken leaves
> Are placed without and velvet moss within.
> And little scraps of grass – and scant and spare
> Of what seems scarce materials, down and hair . . .

Walnut Tree Farm, the home which Roger re-created from abandoned materials, has always reminded me of how men long ago, and maybe even today, had a nest in mind when they looked around for a house. It hides away in foliage which brings secrecy to a vast open common, and going to see him there has often made me think of centuries of spun-out villagers as anxious as Clare to discover what is going on in nests not their own as he was when creeping towards his revered nightingale, terrified that she will hear him and her song be cut short by 'choking fear'. Only a year or two ago I had heard Roger Deakin recording the creaks and bumps of Walnut Tree Farm on the radio, and the rivery sounds of the Waveney, perfect scraps of nature's conversation. Could we hear John Donne's prayer? The one about the house in which there will be 'no noise nor silence, but one equal music ... no ends nor beginnings, but one equal eternity'? And thus we kiss and leave.

Out of the Depths . . .

2nd September

September – in the rain. The cat comes dripping in from long walks in sopping grass to settle down for a long day's sleep. The white Staffordshire figures on the window-sill regard her busy-ness from their stillness. They are on 'The Flight to Egypt' but will never get there. They observe the cat's ablutions, the toes spread out like little fans, the nice gnawing at what is between them, the sudden slumber. On the radio poor young men fall out of the sky on to the wastes of Kandahar. Victoria plums stew on the stove. It is Trinity Twelve. Beyond the window a six-foot spike of great mullein pokes into the sky, its yellow flowers burning their way down its stem.

Today I will re-tell the tale of Jonah at Matins and Even-song. Jesus frequently re-told it, seeing the prophet's three days in the depths of the great fish and his anguished cry, *De profundis!*, as the forerunner of his own descent into Hades. He would have heard this story when he was a boy and would have delighted in it. It only becomes awful when we grow up. 'Go to Nineveh', says God, 'that great city, and cry against it.' 'No fear,' says the prophet. He knows what great cities do to gloomy prophets. Instead, he takes ship from Joppa to Tarshish, happily sailing away from 'the presence of the Lord'. Tolstoy once dodged the Angel of Death, as he thought, by making a long journey to buy a wood, only to find his hotel room turning into a tomb in the middle of the night. His servant outside the door saw nothing, but then he was a teenager. Jonah went to sleep on the ship until the captain woke him up to what was happening to it. It was rocking its way to the bottom of the Mediterranean and all the sailors were shouting to all their gods. The sea demanded a sacrifice so they drew lots and the lot fell on this curious passenger. Down, down, went Jonah into his terrifying salvation. 'This will teach you not to go on a cruise when you are supposed to be doing my work!' God tells him. 'Pity, pity,' begs Jonah. 'You have cast me into the deep . . . All thy billows and waves have passed over me . . . I am cast out of your sight . . . I will pay what I owe you.' Whereupon the great fish puts him ashore, and he makes for Nineveh, gives that wicked place a fright and takes a seat on a hill to enjoy its destruction.

Then comes the most entrancing part of the story. It is a burning sun, not a burning city, which hits Jonah's attention. It is directed on to his head by 'a vehement east wind', and he faints. And this in spite of his taking shelter under a plant. It is a cucurbitaceous plant which produces a gourd and it should have protected Jonah from the fierce sun, only a worm had nibbled it and caused it to wither. 'O Rose, thou art sick . . . The invisible worm . . . has found out thy bed.' God sees that Jonah shows pity for the brief life of a plant 'which came up in a night, and perished in a night', reveals in fact that he is not the hard-hearted person he likes to think he is. Religious vengeance evaporates as God muses, 'should not I spare Nineveh, that great city, if there are more than a hundred and twenty thousand people who cannot discern between their right hand and their left hand, not to mention all the poor animals?'

A vehement south wind roars through the trees on Flower Show day. It seems to be some ten feet above ground, for the late summer flowers scarcely stir. Above is a wildly delicious turmoil as dead wood flies and whirls around.

It is Autumn

15th September

A cluster of friends who knew me, but not each other, have left the earth, or rather have become physically an element of it as their spirits claimed a different alliance, the last being Jane in whose company I clambered around Maiden Castle, and not to be confused with the Jane who so loved an outing. 'Where shall we go?', her small car leaping out of Cambridge. The mid-September readings are from 2 Samuel, that marvellous history of the poet-king David which opens with his threnody on the death of Prince Jonathan, the person he loved most in all the world, and which ends with David buying a threshingfloor on which to build an altar. Thomas Hardy would cycle miles to read what lessons might be drawn from the Books of Samuel and Kings, his mighty influences, in a country church. He translated their wild desires, wickednesses and dramas to Dorset, setting his language alongside that of the Bible, like one of those Loeb Greek–English editions of Homer.

At our village shop I ask for minced beef with which, alongside herbs and onions, I intend to stuff a marrow. Doug, who may be waiting to take the shop dog Gerald for a walk, is appalled. 'Marrow, insipid stuff, I cannot abide it!' Nor, as the conversation continues, can he abide strawberries, raspberries and a good many other delicious things. 'But *blackberries* . . .' His eyes dance. I nobly forsook putting this marrow into the Vegetable and Flower Show, where it would certainly have taken a first prize, in order to devour it – rather like Lady Catherine de Burgh's conviction that her daughter would have been a great pianist had she been taught how to play – and so I return home to wring it off and carry it in triumph to the kitchen. I cut it longways and scrape it into a pair of peeled boats, fill it with hot spicy innards, tie it together with string and settle down to hear it bake. The white cat has to be lifted from the cooker. The radio plays Bruckner's *Te Deum*. While I wait I devour even more Victoria plums, they being guaranteed not to spoil anyone's appetite. A kind of sumptuousness reigns and I find myself mourning those who at this very moment are being driven by starvation into restaurants.

Crack of dawn, well, half-past seven, in the wet garden

with bare feet, considering not what to eat but what to do. First make tea, second have a read. Naked ladies (*Colchicum autumnale*), pure and poisonous, and good for gout, have appeared overnight like mushrooms. Carpets of cyclamen *Neapolitanum album*, the very white rare variety, have just as suddenly carpeted a scrap of hard ground under a guelder rose, and some Himalayan balsam where the thatched barn once stood has grown into delicate trees which sway slightly in the faint wind. Six quinces hang in a group. And here are the secateurs, lost a month ago, gently rusting away. And here comes Duncan searching for Ginny the runaway dog. And on the News there is much mourning for lost childhood and much talk about how to prise the young from their screens, that Pied Piper which has long whisked them out of sight. For the first time in its history no child plays in the village street, no outside games are sung.

They are still mending the church tower, but slowly. Now we wait to have Tudor bricks made for Sir William's finials, and which he probably put there in order to delight him as he stared up the hill from Smallbridge Hall – and of course to the glory of God. They are costing us a pretty fortune.

The Charterhouse Dandelions

26th September

To London with Christopher for the Lambeth Gathering, that pleasant get-together at the Charterhouse. The Master, James Thomson, greets us. The Dean of Canterbury shuffles the notes which he doesn't need for his architectural sermon, the Brothers are hospitable and witty in the way old men are when released from having to be serious, and the bricks and mortar, not only of this once monastery-mansion-school now grand shelter for the aged, as well as all London, burn with late warmth as they decay. Charterhouse Square, Carthusian Street, and hints of the Grande-Chartreuse itself, make me long to wander about in the September sunshine and re-apply a World War Two poem by Alun Lewis to what I feel:

> Softly the civilised
> Centuries fall,
> Paper on paper,
> Peter on Paul . . .

No leaves down yet. Unless the new gardener at the Charterhouse has wielded his new broom. The great trees hang with fire. Listening to a lecture on the Duke of Norfolk who turned this holy place into his palace, my eye traces a complex scene of a perfectly faded Flemish tapestry which hangs near me. Gods and goddesses as one would expect, but dandelions? James I arrived in this room after his long ride from Scotland. Did he stare around and say to himself, 'Yes, Apollo, maybe, and a boy with a hobby-horse certainly, but dandelions?' What I wondered was, as I frequently do, how did these Tudor magnates reconcile their turning of holy places into their spectacular seats? Dean Willis's sermon returned us to the mind of the Middle Ages as the temples arose, to a sacred geometry concealed by our 'Perp' and 'Dec' etc. We sing Cowper's 'Jesus, wher'er thy people meet', which he wrote especially for Matins in a drawing-room, the church being repaired. Back home with the commuters, the setting sun in my eyes all the way, below Colchester station, the meadows which were Camulodunon. Our day tickets are seized by the machine, our car bumps down the track, our day out is over. The white cat is starving. The post is filled with the gaze of hungry children.

And now there is harvest festival, three of them to be exact, and Phyllida will be bringing the sheaves saved from the instant grind of the combine, and there will be the practical tins for St Saviour's Hospice and the Harvest Loaf of course for the altar. Harvest festivals are weird celebrations these days, with almost no one in the village having done so much as a hand's turn in the fields and probably half the village unable to tell wheat from barley. 'But there you are!' as the bellringer says. Now and then, in my sermons, I enquire, 'Where are we?' Politely, of course. 'Who are we?'

I sit reading outside in the nice hot afternoon, the cat's head on the page, the woodpecker rattling overhead, the beautiful vapour trails of the Stansted planes curling over the horizon. The last of the balsam is going pop. The stream sings its trickling song. Now and then a good idea for a story strikes me and I instantly dismiss it. Why spoil a perfect sloth? I think of tennis players, not Andy Murray, but poor young Lord Surrey listening to the sound of racquet and ball outside his cell as he awaits execution – he whose blank verse pattern would be used by Shakespeare.

Bellwether Talk

29th September

Just down the road they are holding an exhibition of Gainsborough's dogs, those much loved animals of his which demanded just as much attention from his brush as, say, the Duchess of Devonshire. And then, over the Welsh border, from which I have just returned, they were holding an exhibition of Seren Bell's portraits of sheep. And of course these were the kind of likenesses none of us expected to see in a frame. I slowly passed sheep's face to sheep's face, each time meeting the artist's truthful picture of her sitter's individuality. But there is a corporate melancholy, a heavy-lidded sadness, an expressive eye from which I had to turn away. 'Why us for your religious imagery?' these creatures asked. 'Why since you obviously find so many species lovelier, brighter and nobler than a sheep, why do you see your Lord in us?'

The sheep artist, driving under the Black Mountains, would brake now and then when a grazing Suffolk or Cheviot caught her attention. Its features in the portrait will not be theological, simply that of a sheep, but it will ask big questions. A question like 'O Lamb of God, which taketh away the sin of the world, have mercy upon us.' Or, 'Little lamb, who made thee?' Or, 'Full grown sheep, why is your wool, once the wealth of the nation, now worth less than the shearer's wages?' But most of all the question will be, 'Why have I never really seen your face until it appeared in an art gallery?' And what a good face it is, sagacious, peaceful and ultimately tragic.

Visitors from Dorset arrive, thus more sheepish talk. Would it not have been unlikely that Farmer Oak's flock in *Far from the Madding Crowd* have so conveniently destroyed itself for the convenience of the plot by jumping to its death, all 200 members of it? And all led to this end by their leader's bell? This sheep was called the bellwether. Those who blindly follow a human bellwether will in all probability come to the abyss. One of the Dorset visitors longs to see a sheep's bell and there is one in the big wooden box of all sorts in the larder. It needs listening to. Immensely ancient, it clunks musically when I shake it. It is a sound from a lost countryside, earthy, archaic, and not unlike some old bell for the Elevation. Its tongue hung out and its sides were still parpolished by fleece. Thomas Hardy said that the note of a sheep-bell was like the ticking of a clock to country people, and reminded us that its ring changes were caused by the animal's feeding or running. Gabriel Oak heard it like a firebell heralding total disaster. No longer his own man, he descended into a common labourer.

Aaron the priest was a bellwether. His people made him 'holy garments . . . for glory and beauty' which were hemmed all along with 'a golden bell and a pomegranate, a golden bell and a pomegranate'. Other than some horse-bells in Zechariah, Aaron's are the only bells mentioned in the Old Testament. Like sheep, his little nation flocked in his wake as he walked to the sacred place. And thus the pastoral vision began, wandering through Jewish history until a young man, down by the Jordan, cried, 'Here comes the Lamb of God! Follow him!' Here was the divine Bellwether, one who would see us safe.

Fat sheep appeared and re-appeared in the Powys mists like moving pearls. They munch in and out of my view, eating their brief lives away. No bell to lead them. They spread themselves over Offa's Dyke, hoping to catch an artist's eye.

The Death of Children

5th October

October mornings are doubly black as rivery mists and sunlessness gradually part company, creating degrees of opacity. At first, or at 5 a.m. say, nothing is visible from the north windows – the same north windows whose light fell on John Nash's easel – and I am unable to make out as much as a great tree. Then comes the soft unveiling of the familiar view. Daylight forces the mist to take colour, to thin itself, to let me see through it at actualities beyond it, just as George Herbert said we should see beyond the unsubstantial artistry of coloured glass in churches and recognise the glorious realities which they can only suggest. Landscape artists begin a work by blocking in the major objects which stretch before them. October dawns work this way. First the featureless void, then the murky outlines of what this particular view must contain, then, gradually, gradually, all that exists on the other side of the pane. The birds, those that have not decamped to Africa, call out. It is a new day. A beam wavers and sweeps along Garnon's Chase, stripping oak after oak of its remnant cover as Tom's car twists towards the station. If I stood in the drenched grass outside I might hear, faraway like moneyed sirens, the faint screams of the commuter trains.

A scholar has sent me his take on a John Clare poem 'Graves of Infants'. Simultaneously in the press I read about the Pope's having to deal with Limbo. Look up Limbo. Oh my goodness. 'Those in limbo are excluded from supernatural beatitude, but according to St Thomas Aquinas enjoy full natural happiness. The existence of limbo is a matter of theological opinion on which the Church has never pronounced definitely either way.' But then we come to *limbus infantium* – unbaptised babies who although born in original sin are innocent of personal guilt. In fact, although many a child was too ill to make the font, it would have had the midwife's sign of the cross on its forehead and her speedy, 'In the name of the Father . . .' the minute it emerged, infant mortality and her grubby hands being what they were. 'Limbo . . . mumbo-jumbo . . .' murmured a voice on the radio. I suppose that the Church does have to now and then turn out its medieval attic. However, here comes John Clare, father of nine, survivor of twins and sanest of poets where children and what we now dub ecology are concerned. Rural religion and economics have frequently shown their madness when we compare them to what he believed.

In 'Graves of Infants' he enters the vast sadness of nine-teenth-century child mortality. You raised some, you lost some, they said. Victorian literature is full of what most families experienced, the deathbeds of boys and girls. Country churchyards are full of children – city ones too, of course. Should a child die now it shakes the entire parish. By disease or accident, it is unnatural to us. But not long ago it was entirely natural, for nature itself was tragic, as Clare knew all too terribly. In June 1844, from Northampton Asylum – his 'Mad House' – came his reconciling conclusion to the common fate of many children. It was the only answer which he could make sense of. Brief life or long life, it was no more than aspects of nature:

God is their parent, they need no tear . . .
A bud their life-time, and a flower their close . . .
All prayers are needless – beads they need not tell;
White flowers their mourners are, nature their passing bell.

Warden Pears and Samoa

18th October

St Luke's day. The sun has gone, the warmth remains. Soft rains soak the turning leaves. Violets are in bloom beneath a sheltering shrub. An old Warden pear-tree fell flat in July. Once I had to wait until its fruit tumbled down but now I bend to pick it. Tree and pears are doing well, as is the ivy which brought them low. In Thomas Hardy's grim poem, the Ivy-Wife describes her fate when the ash she lusted after 'Being bark-bound, flagged, snapped, fell outright, / And in his fall felled me!' Once my pear-tree has been picked I will divorce it from its ivy-wife and try to prop it back into its rightful towering state. Warden pears are cookers. You chop them in half, do not peel them, and bake them in a covered dish with cloves and wine. Then you eat them for a month. King Henry IV had them at his wedding.

On Sunday afternoon Ian, Joachim from Berlin and I did the village round in the October heatwave. The sun was burning the sugar-beet mountains down at Garnons. The fields were empty and wondering what to do next. There was a raggedy sugar-beet aftermath, a few basking birds and a staring sky. We plodded along, mile after mile, noting small things. Lots of summer flowers but in meagre patches. The Suffolk side of the Stour, vide Hardy again, was how he described Emma's gown – 'air-blue'. We encountered Harry and Paul 'tiffling' about, lugging dead wood from a hollow. We saw the mere, secretive as ever, its surface white and motionless. Sopping grass wet us to the knees. We spoke of Robert Louis Stevenson and of writers full of books who had little time to live, and of his busy gaiety as stories and travel essays sailed from Samoa to the London publishers. How the rains clanged and clattered on his corrugated iron mansion! How quinine kept the ink flowing! And the surprising post-scripts to the letters. 'Give my love to Henry James.' And here we are, tramping past Neil's cottage to which I meant to bring some old folksongs, only I forgot. Neil sings songs at our harvest feast, translating himself back into the nineteenth century, face and all.

Religion is having a bad press as a mainly secularised society wades into its emblems, and politicians begin to draw up plans for a more uniform nation. Dress codes from the Middle Ages squabble with dress codes from Marks and Spencer. The Stevensons in Samoa are waited on by twenty servants of both sexes, and both beautiful, clad only in what he calls 'kilts', coming as he does from Edinburgh. He poor man is skin and bone, and coughing. Also mildly Presbyterian.

Confident European missionaries boss everybody about. But monarch of all is Tusitala, the teller of tales. Everyone, Christian or not, wears bangles. They slide on Stevenson's thin arms. German sailors arrive from the harbour, put on their best whites and do a dance. Death waits for the rain to stop. Down below, after the war ceases, they sort out decapitated heads.

A PCC tonight. Apologies for Absence, Matters Arising, the New Sound System, Churchyard Trees, School Governors, the Administration of the Chalice, the black valley outside, the familiar arguments and me inwardly wondering whether I am moderate or Laodicean. Laodicea was a lovely Hellenistic city and a bishopric, a thoughtful kind of place I have always imagined, and not tepid as St Paul said. A place for neither the fanatic nor the irreligious.

Richard Mabey and Michael Mayne

23rd October

The great autumn garden tidy-up has come to a sopping end. Also, the brogues in which I have walked England, Scotland and Wales for many years now let in water. I surveyed my wet socks with amazement but when I took the shoes to the menders the young man said, 'Chuck 'em away.' Then, seeing my shocked face, he added, 'Fill the toes up with Superglue.' So I went to buy a new pair from a shop which had a hundred different shoes for women and four for men. And so home, as Pepys would have said. The windscreen wipers squelched and screamed, and the wheels threw up rainbows. Rooks flew low and a little sun went in and out. The Long Walk is covered in mast and the broken fungi which the badgers have nosed then disdained.

To Diss to see Richard Mabey, whose kitchen garden is bursting with food. There is a single primrose in flower, just as, back at Bottengoms Farm, violets are in bloom beneath a bush. Warming planets provide guilty joys. We ramble along in a featureless landscape which because it has nothing brave to show us is brimming with interest. Here are the first few miles of Norfolk, with here and there some old and new barns, some once headland oaks, some highways going to grass, some isolated birds, some fast-running ditches. Heavens, how well one feels. And the ease of friendships which run back to the year dot. The comfort of them, the catching up. Some of the fields are greening, with winter wheat, some barren and showing off their rained-on flints like onyx. Richard is writing about beeches. I don't know what I am writing about but must soon make up my mind. We turn south otherwise we would be tramping to Norwich. There is a leafless apple-tree like a Samuel Palmer apple-tree, all blissful with fruit, and there is the train home. The skies empty themselves over Stowmarket. Such a downpour, it blinds the carriage windows. The commuters look down, not out, softly tapping their keys. Ipswich is Niagara Falls, Colchester – well. My track, goodness! Although having gone beyond mere drenching, a deliciousness makes itself felt. And there, crazily, sits the white cat under the John Clare rose faithfully waiting for me like the faithful hound on the Victorian battlefield who guards the body of his dead master.

What can one do with an heroic cat? I dry her and feed her before drying myself. Two can play at that game. During the night the rain cradles the old house, whooshing around its wall, overwhelming its guttering, sieving its way through the ivy. The Epistle of James presents rain as an example of patience. The fruit of the earth, the first and second coming of Christ, have to be created by early and late rains.

Michael Mayne has gone to God. He has been in my head throughout these wild October days. We first met when he was Vicar of Great St Mary's, Cambridge, and from then on, at Westminster and Salisbury, he and Alison were part of my life. He was a passionate reader. Amongst so many things he was able to give a language to suffering which complemented that of medicine. In this he was a layman of genius. All the diseases should be presented in a dual language. Michael was an autobiographer of two still mysterious illnesses, ME and cancer, allowing us to see further into them, and into the common business of living and dying, than anyone I have ever known. And all this plus Traherne's adoration of simply being on this beautiful earth.

In October

24th October

Coming home on the Saturday bus from the new Dean's installation at St Edmundsbury with old ladies rocking to and fro with their shopping, and Lavenham tower jumping about in the autumn fields, first this side, then the other, but never straight ahead. The new Dean has come from Exeter where, I believe, they have the oldest cat-flap in England. Our cathedral was filled to the brim, such a beautiful collected song of praise, and it having set up little screens in the Quire I was able to see for the first time what was going on in the nave. Outside, the tea-tent billowed. Inside Dean Neil preached his first sermon – on hope. There was a Latin song to our poor young Edmund, crowned at fifteen, murdered at thirty, and 'Who for Christ's dear name in this world / Pain and tribulation bore'. On the way in Bishop Richard and I talked about R. S. Thomas and his truthful confession of a sometimes absent God. Also what it must have been like to go to church in Manafon and find *him* in the pulpit! I actually did sit in this church a long time ago, although not on a Sunday. So I was safe, or endangered in another sense.

A poetry editor is coming to lunch so I shake down the last of the Victorias for dessert. They thump in the dying orchard grass, now and then sending a wasp on its way. I gather late flowers and scrub my own potatoes, and pick fennel for the fish. South-westerlies continue to warm the valley, so I plan a little walk. Not too far. It is St Matthew's day, old Money-bags, as our ancestors saw him, forgetting his immediate leap away from the seat of custom when he heard, 'Follow me.' People's lives are still crudely simplified by the tools of their trade. 'What do you do?' a stranger would ask at some party. This when I was a youthful poet. 'I work for a publisher', I would sometimes reply, as vaguely as I could, and hoping that this would shut them up.

They have spread nets over the cricket pitch in order for it to grow grass for football, and somebody tells me that they are going to Wales for Christmas 'to get away from our families'. But what of the meantime? What of these four blessed months ending in 'ber' which, now that the Clean Air Act has unveiled their loveliness, have become for me a kind of toiling happiness? Let them take their time. Let them drag, even. Let them say, check the oil tank, buy some new jerseys, fill up the log space, make you think. Let them bring you yet another birthday, if they must. Only now and then do I catch *Thought for the Day*. I like the Sikh one, and the Rector of Putney's one, and Rabbi Blue's one – 'I now find public worship too rich, so now, I just say. "Come to me, dear Friend".' He often sounds like one of those Christian Jews in the Upper Room. Faith is a wonderfully entangling tree. When Abraham rested himself under a tree on the plains of Mamre he could not have imagined where its roots would spread.

My tall oaks – they are actually Duncan's – shower down corn and twigs, and when I mow the long lawn they rattle and ping, and fly about in an irritable manner. Pigs should be snuffling them up, not my grass-box. To think that had I lived here centuries ago I would have rights of pannage. Or would they be Duncan's rights of pannage to be charitably passed on to me? Weekend walkers crunch along. Bell-practice begins. Imprisoned children watch their mouse. The river is nicely full and Harry has a new herd, bull and all. To think – it is autumn! O blessed days.

Colin, Master Book-mender

15th November

Was there ever such a delectable autumn. I am playing Last Across with the geraniums and the marvellous spire of yucca blossom, leaving them outside until the first rumours of frost. Hazel and ash leaves sail over them, through them. Thinning trees let in pale shafts of morning light. Fungus rots at their roots. The air is both morbid and sublime. I find it hard to stay in. Books topple in the study, paper stays wordless, gobble-de-gook messages remain uninterpreted on the answer-phone. Like the flowers, I must make the most of it, this St Martin's big summer. He was an army officer whose feast falls on 11th November but he suddenly proclaimed himself a conscientious objector – 'I am Christ's soldier; I am not allowed to fight.' He was hugely active, hugely right, excitingly important. On his day the poppy petals fall on the young faces in the Albert Hall.

Colin the farmer's son arrives to say goodbye with new-laid eggs and some mushrooms he has gathered en-route from Maltings Farm to Bottengoms Farm, a tramp of half a mile. He and his wife are seeing the world before settling down. That is, he is mending ancient books in Adelaide. He is a master-restorer of old volumes. Bindings, foxed pages, collapsed texts, dim illustrations are healed by him. But he gets homesick. Australia is a curiously homesick-making country, I found – although no land could be more unlike England. It is deep in drought at this minute. It is a place of harsh renewals. Strangely, talking to Colin, pressing on him something to read on the long haul, I find myself visitor-sick for a glimpse of the blue gums and blue water below my brother's house near Sydney. I am in that very English room once more. There is the marble fireplace in which fires are never lit. There are the piles of books on English gardens and English cathedrals. There are the prints of Suffolk. There, in the hallway, is the larger than life brass rubbing of Sir Robert de Bures from Acton, our birthplace, irritable in his armour and in his isolation.

Now and then I steer my way down the mile-long track late at night. Darker and darker it becomes until, as I feel my steps entering the orchard, there is a kind of crescendo of the old rural darkness, an opacity which is almost palpable, hanging from my body as it moves through the fruit trees. Most villages possessed this blessed darkness until a few years ago. But now they are told not to bear it, to regard it as a danger, to wage war against it. Darkness is good for you, this natural daily absence of the sun, that is. Its artificial destruction in the countryside itself is a tragedy. Forget its religious and social symbolism, return to its naturalness. Feel it on your skin. Let it become a part of your wakefulness as well as your sleep. The visionary American poet Theodore Roethke said that even just philosophically 'In a dark time, the eye begins to see'. Physically the loss of each day's darkness is one we should not endure.

St Martin's summer notwithstanding, birds, beasts and insects are taking flight, laying in supplies, making beds. At dusk a river of rooks flowed overhead, and a badger crossed the lane. At dawn a pair of bluetits fed wildly on berries with something of the fervour of a crisp-gorging woman who sat opposite to me on the train. Stuff, stuff, for the hungry day must come. Frosts too.

The Music Girl

22nd November

The sumptuous November days continue. Golden leaves hide the lawns, particularly those from the hedge hazels. Rain-water stays in the ruts. The ponds are glassy, the skies aquamarine and noisy with homing birds. Now and then a drenched fox or rabbit lopes across the greening field where the winter wheat is showing. A solitary figure descends the church tower to pack up, his task done. The time-wrecked finials which Sir William fancifully placed on its corners when Shakespeare was writing *All's Well that Ends Well* have been replaced. Now all that is needed is fifty years' weather to blend them into the scenery. John, our Admirable Crichton, has also come down from on high, having taken advantage of the scaffolding to paint the clock. I watch these conclusions from where I am brushing lichen from John Nash's gravestone where in less than thirty years his name struggles to be read. Whereas on the grand neighbouring tombs of the Constables the deeply cut inscriptions continue to defy botany. The churchyard is a great untidy bed of seared yellow coverings through which the dead poke their names and pleas, yet again.

It is the feast of St Cecilia. I mention her at Matins. She was first buried in the cemetery of St Callistus on the Aurelian Way, this long ago girl who 'sang to God in her heart', sharing ground with a pope who had done time in a Sardinian quarry. But now she has her own church of St Cecilia in Trastevere, where a statue shows her, naturally if unusually, lying on her side, sound asleep. There she is, say all the composers, this remote person from whom traditionally flows the Church's glorious music. What would she have made of the BBC's *Songs of Praise*, I wonder? Had she composed a hymn they would not have mentioned her name. They first celebrated Cecilia at a service in London in which Purcell's *Te Deum* and *Jubilate in D* were sung. Then, a century or so later, came the Cecilian Movement itself for the reform of Roman Catholic church music. Now and then we 'hear her', as it were, singing in a quire window silently, as she nurses her emblem, a toy organ. 'What passion *cannot* Music raise and quell?' asked John Dryden in his 'Ode' to her. We sang, 'My tongue shall never tire of chanting with the choir', I hope truthfully.

On Wednesday the Powys contingent bumped down the old track, old friends from the Welsh border. I lit an ash-log fire to welcome them. I remember their tiny church at Discoed. It would have been a kneeling place for medieval shepherds. The poet Edward Storey has these past few years refilled it with singing. We have lunch at the pub in Nayland, leaving the car on the hard where John Constable's father's barges dumped coal and anything else which travelled easier by river than by road. The weather then started to become a bit wild, or less serene, and the willows thrashed about and there was a mighty rustling. 'More what you expect, like,' said a pleased old chap. Exactly. I thought of the reduced light of Radnorshire, how it is diffused, how it avoids brilliance.

Whereas the light in East Anglia avoids nothing. It just pours down like one of those gifts from St James's Father of lights, no matter if the sun is in. Thus the Stour goes on gleaming in its sullen fashion as the days darken.

What to tell them on Sunday? Parables, poetry and history flicker across the flimsy pages. There are two kings, reminds the Lectionary, Edmund and Christ. Also there is Isaac Watts, hymnwriter, d. 1748. And there is Stir-up Sunday. But how about the young Saviour standing on the Temple steps listening to the singing and joining in?

Ditching

10th December

I revel in this April in December, having set aside for the moment such spoilsport realities as global warming. I am ditching, letting the clean water flow foot by foot. The bank is piled high with chopped blackberry, elder, hazel. Bundled in old sweaters, I splosh along. As with all manual labour, the stream of consciousness provides its accompaniment. Irritants and blisses float on its surface, bobbing against each other. Why are some broadcast church services so rehearsed, so martinet? All those barked Amens, all those hymns with the private feeling wrung from them. And, now that I am on the subject (some decidedly wintry water having entered my awareness) what is actually *happening* in *Songs of Praise*? What does the singer know when for the third time he mouths with all his might, 'Shout, as you journey on'? Or even 'Hail with united voice'? If only Bishop Ambrose were alive. I hank weed from the horse-pond and a robin occupies the dribbling mass. It really is the most enchanting afternoon. My wellingtons make nice sucking sounds and my best garden gloves are liquid balls. It is warm – almost sultry. The geraniums are flowering all over again.

Meanwhile, off-stage where I am concerned at this moment, the school is putting on *Baboushka* in the village hall and attending woodland classes with the Suffolk Wildlife Trust, and Barry is pleading for new bellringers. 'The average age of the Wormingford ringers is sixty-six years.' Parish councillors and school governors are needed. What am I doing in a ditch? Having a rest. Angels and birds take turns to fill my head. First Raphael then a pheasant, both wonderfully plumed. Each with a lot to say. When the hedge parts I can see girls wrapping their horses up in blankets for the winter. Too soon, too soon. The ditch has changed its muddy ways. Its bed is crystal clear and glittering with shingle. It tinkles like a xylophone and looks unseasonably chilly. Fragments of farm breakages are washed out from its bright flow like gold-dust. What a row there must have been when someone dropped that teapot. The angels and birds having sung their last song, I listen to ghostly plough-horses filling up after the day's work, drawing the entire pond into them, their feet sinking deeper and deeper into the Advent mulch, the ploughman's too. What he would have said about ditching in December only heaven knew. The white cat makes a fastidious appearance to announce starvation, and 'You'll get your death'. True. Who won't?

Maggie comes to lunch and she talks about her New Zealand

girlhood, and about her parents, and about Katherine Mansfield fighting off TB so as to get on with her stories. Whenever someone starts discussing Katherine Mansfield – or it might be her hero Chekhov or any writer – I long to dash to the bookcase and start re-reading them, usually with a marvellous sensation of never having read them before. Even when I myself have written about them long ago. So many of them, like Katherine Mansfield, hadn't a minute to spare. No time to dig ditches and muse on birds and angels. No time for the school's production of *Baboushka*, and certainly no time to ring bells. With some Chardonnay from Chile to help us, Maggie and I put the Church of England to rights. We are having long lives. So many wild Decembers, though so few without frosts. My garden-rags steam by the boiler. The wind rises and wants to come in, pushing against the windows, bawling down the chimney.

The Finial-maker

Advent Sunday

The splendours of the season have been held back to the very last minute. Now, on the very eve of Advent, what a showing! The air is ablaze with falling leaves, each one of them a lively flame. In *Paradise Lost*, Milton sees the dark angels of Satan's army 'thick as autumnal leaves that strow the brooks / In Vallombrosa', so what brought such an image into his head as he lay blind in Buckinghamshire? Did the rustling beech leaves outside his cottage suddenly bring back his youthful travels in Italy? Poets and artists have frequently recorded the touching innocence of soldiers resting before battle. In *Paradise Lost* Satan and his dark angels have a terrible beauty.

I plunge along the river-bed which was a lane before the rain fell on it. I pass the several-yards-around oak which would have been shedding leaves when Milton was living. A slender young ash shelters beside it. Both have their feet in a stream, as does a crooked telegraph pole, the one which Christopher wants when it finally tumbles. Blanketed horses watch me with jewelled eyes. The skies are dramatic, black as sin one side, golden gates the other, and seagulls change colour as they fly north or west. Cars on the main road are blinded by the sunset. But walkers are illumined in outline like Benedictine saints on a medieval altarpiece. Now and then a sightless driver honks to draw my attention and I wave. But to whom? Wrens scatter in the bare hawthorn, flying through the rocking thorns without getting pierced, travelling along with me but never leaving the hedge. In the village I dwell on the death of someone I didn't know but who, all the same, is not a stranger. For this is what happens in small communities and congregations. I actually find death less and less sad. It is the getting to it which grieves the heart.

The collect for Advent Sunday is marvellously Miltonic. 'Almighty God, give us grace that we may cast away the works of darkness, and put upon us the armour of light, now in the time of this mortal life, in which thy son Jesus Christ came to visit us in great humility . . .' What perfection of language for the divine approach. And to be followed by St Paul's 'therefore love is the fulfilling of the law'. I stand in the dank grass to chat with the solitary craftsman who for these past weeks has replaced the Tudor finials of our Saxon tower. His long curls are tied back with a ribbon, like the Scarlet Pimpernel's, and for weeks he has toiled in a whirl of horse-chestnut leaves and through this autumn's storms and heats, the rich red spiky corners emerging like works of art under his hands. Who taught him how to make Tudor brick finials? Or to be so happy doing it? And what did the church rooks think as they cawed over him in their hundreds, and the Valley starlings in their thousands? And now it is done. No need to touch these bricks for another 500 years, never mind diocesan architects, etc. I praise this fine repair in my annual Thank you speech at the bell ringers' dinner at the Crown. I urge the ringers to look up past the old bells, beyond what they know. Which is what we must all do in Advent, and in order that we may rise to the life immortal. Back home the lawns rest under leafy carpets and will do so for a while yet. This meeting of growth with ending is the year's annual wish. David shuffles his way through it with apples, Chilver's Delight, Egremont Russet, the latter 'recorded by Mr J. Scott in Somerset in 1872'. There's a date for a diary!

Alternative Hosts

20th December

For years my Christmas would alternate between Cornwall and Suffolk, between poet and painter. And their hard-cooking wives of course. These Christmases were not a bit alike. The poet took me to the Midnight in a freezing granite church, the painter gave me a drop of 'the crature' and a candle and saw me off to bed. Their ancient houses were hot in parts and full of drowsy cats. The poet was James Turner and the artist John Nash. I never recovered from the shock, or shall we say the bitter disappointment, of seeing Catherine Turner standing on Bodmin Road station at seven in the evening, once in the snow, and a good twenty miles from her oven, all smiles and kisses certainly, but with that jolly promise of a great feed tomorrow when I was starving today. Whereas when John Nash picked me up at Colchester Station in his Triumph Herald, an ashtray on wheels, I knew that the festive gluttony would begin the moment we stepped through the door. The Turners had a turkey and the Nashes had a goose. The Turners put all their cards up, the Nashes about a dozen, leaving all the rest in the Shoebox. It was possible to be put up one year and demoted to the Shoebox the next, although impossible to know why. The Nashes' present was either wildly extavagant, a drawing, or a shilling mug. The poet and I exchanged our latest books.

But the lasting wonder of these different Christmases remains richly embedded in the Boxing Day walk, which would be by two very different seas. Not that John Nash cared much for walking, so I usually found some addict of the shingle ridge which stretched from Orford to Aldeburgh to accompany me in the crunching, gusty turmoil, our eyes down, our clothes useless, mere windbags blowing round our poor naked flesh. In Cornwall this walk would take place along the vast golden curve of Constantine Bay. Should we pass other couples walking it off – the turkey or goose – the

Suffolk ones would commiserate via a gesture. They had been driven from the house by their savage children, by the television, by the sheer mess. The Cornish post-revellers on the other hand tended to be, like myself, more visitor than family, and were thus less crushed by domestic guilt. They waved and shouted, and bounded along with their hosts' dogs, picked up shells and expressed joy.

I beachcombed in both places. Pushing against the wall of sea air, battling on, I very soon became entranced by the mightiness of the Atlantic Ocean or the North Sea, granting them their grandeur and mesmeric force. Really making the most of them, as I did when I was a child from an inland scene. On one side of the Boxing Day walk was this vast natural object, on the other was the minutiae which it strewed in my path, the tide-worn objects called flotsam and jetsam, the driftwood, wrack and marvellous stones which were fabulous when under water and nothing to boast about when dry, the fragments of wooden or plastic boats – mostly the latter these days – and the rags and tatters of summer, a T-shirt, a sandal, a towel, a wine bottle. The Cornish artists Wilhemina Barnes-Graham and Margaret Mellis, and the Essex artist Guy Taplin turned wreckage into seabirds.

Dancing in a Ring

23rd December

Percy Dearmer wanted carols to be sung at church services throughout the year. Instead of the anthem, for instance, and as an extra delight after the blessing, now that the choir and congregation were in good voice. He described them as 'songs with a religious impulse that are simple, hilarious, popular and modern'. 'Please, sir, may we sing a carol?' begged a member of Parson Woodforde's congregation on Christmas morning. 'You may but not until I am out of the church.' Some remote intelligence presumably told him that a carol was a dance. Or maybe, his *Diary* revealing his appetite, he flinched from having to listen to the eating and drinking carols of his day such as 'Wassail, wassail, all over the town!'

Our carol services – Henry takes one, I take the other – have to be the same every year, though different, his at Little Horkesley, mine at Wormingford. They must begin with Mrs Alexander and end with Charles Wesley. I religiously destroy each year's copy so as to hold on to a mite of freshness in the latest selection and I am always startled, as is everyone else, by the heart-wrenching power of the familiar. Into its English gothic seting comes a Bethlehem so at variance with the grim concrete town we see on the screen that it is hard to find a connection. Out goes all debate. The wonder, the wonder! And all of it just saved in time. For if Cecil Sharp and Ralph Vaughan Williams, two young men, had not suddenly realised just before World War One that a rare kind of song was slipping into silence, the carol-book would have been a flimsy affair. I love the secular borrowings such as Bishop Brooks's 'O little town of Bethlehem' being sung to Vaughan Williams's tune of 'The Ploughboy's Dream'. As for Gustav Holst's setting of Christina Rossetti's 'In the bleak mid-winter', the chancel arch shivers as we do our best to re-enter poverty.

'Where do Christmas songs begin?' asks Timothy Dudley-Smith. 'By the stable of an inn / where the songs of hosts on high / mingled with a baby's cry.' Where do Christmas songs hit the roof? In King's College Chapel. Borrowed from Truro Cathedral, the Festival of Nine Lessons and Carols was first heard at Cambridge in December 1918 in a world of mourning, in a tall church of empty stalls. In a sacred cage where, to adapt Shakespeare, once the sweet birds sang. Now all shot and buried in mud. Come, thou Redeemer of the earth. I strew nine lesson readers through the lectern Bible. No names, By their deeds shall ye know them. A churchwarden, a hospice director, a farmer, a bellringer, a commuter, a schoolboy, a schoolgirl, a parish councillor, a lay canon. Then I hand the whole thing over to Christopher the organist and wait for the village to swarm in. Which it usually does. Waiting, I remember learning Frances Chesterton's 'How far is it to Bethlehem?', from mother, I suppose, and definitely from the curate's wife, a large Welshwoman with a surprisingly small, true voice, 'Lullay my liking, my dear son, my sweeting; Lullay my dear heart, mine own dear darling!', and other carols which remain outside our nine. As is Geoffrey Shaw's robust 'Unto us a boy is born!' Carols are filled with exclamation marks. Our handbell ringers stand round a table and make a silvery noise, the Advent candles burn out. There is the crib, invented they say by St Francis, ours with knitted creatures, human and farmyard. There is the gale outside and the music within.